The Art of the Family Tree

QUARRY

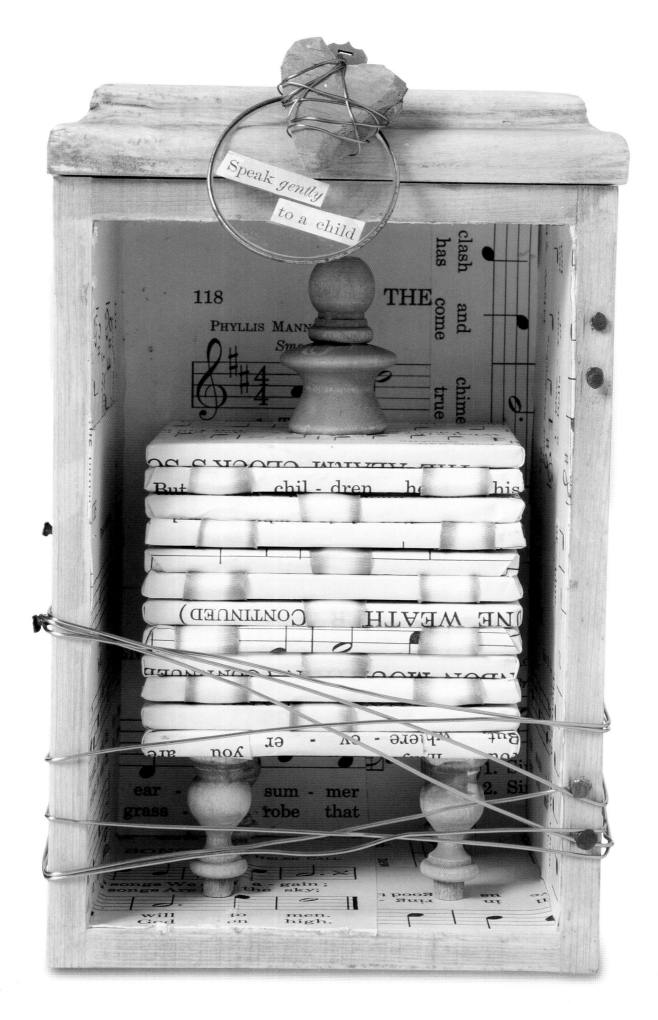

GLOUCESTER MASSACHUSETTS

QUARRY BOOKS

THE ART OF THE *Family Tree*

Creative Family History Projects Using Paper Art, Fabric & Collage

JENN MASON

FOREWORD BY PATRICIA BOLTON, EDITOR-IN-CHIEF,
QUILTING ARTS MAGAZINE AND *CLOTH PAPER SCISSORS*

First published in the United States of America by
Quarry Books, a member of
Quayside Publishing Group
33 Commercial Street
Gloucester, Massachusetts 01930-5089
Telephone: (978) 282-9590
Fax: (978) 283-2742
www.quarrybooks.com

Library of Congress Cataloging-in-Publication Data
Mason, Jenn.
    The art of the family tree : creative family history projects using paper art, fabric, and
collage / Jenn Mason.
        p.   cm.
    Includes bibliographical references.
    ISBN-13: 978-1-59253-339-8
    ISBN-10: 1-59253-339-6
1. Photograph albums. 2. Family in art. 3. Genealogy. I. Title.
TR501.M368 2007
745.593—dc22   2006100293
                                                                       CIP

ISBN-13: 978-1-59253-339-8
ISBN-10: 1-59253-339-6

10 9 8 7 6 5 4 3 2 1

Design: Dawn DeVries Sokol
Cover Image: Allan Penn
Illustrations: Jenn Mason
Templates: Melanie Powell, Shy Buck Studios

Printed in Singapore

Mother love is the fuel that enables
a normal human being to do the impossible.
—Marion C. Garretty

To Mum, *for whatever you did to make me whatever I am.*

CONTENTS

Watercolor Tree variation, page 41

Ancestral Star Book, page 48

Collaged Canvas, page 34

Fabric Journal Collection Book, page 54

Foreword

Every family has one: the genealogist. That relative who spends hours chained to the dining room table, hunkered over a patchwork spread of yellowing birth certificates, century-old love letters, and creased, sepia-toned photographs in efforts to uncover the mysteries of the family and answer that age-old question: How did we come to be?

In my clan, the fervent archeologist of family files would be my grandmother, Anne Bassett Stanley Chatham. Daughter of a former U.S. congressman and governor of the Commonwealth of Virginia, my grandmother is a proud citizen of the Old Dominion State—but she's a granny with her secrets. When her father was in Congress (and she just a slip of a thing boarding at an all-girl high school) she eloped with my humor-loving, thrill-seeking grandfather, a hillbilly from the mountains of North Carolina. She wasn't the first to breathe a bit of scandal into the family and though she and my grandfather enjoyed nearly fifty years of marital bliss before he passed, she decided to research the family tree and see who else had their stories to tell. That was the early '70s, and twenty-five years later she self-published a hardcover book that is a whopping 1,246 pages.

Complete with multiple fold-outs of ancestral pedigree charts (some dating back to the 1200s), maps, migration trails, copies of photographs, newspaper clippings, obituaries, birth certificates, hand-written wills, love letters, and applications to the Colonial Dames XVII Century, it rivals the weight, word count, and width of an unabridged dictionary. If I flip open the book, I'll stumble upon any number of interesting stories or bits of text. There's an entire chapter entitled, "When Individuals Go Against the Norm," for example. And here's a passage from "Chicken for Supper," a letter written by a homesick soldier to his wife during World War II:

We couldn't understand how such a fine-looking bird could make such a poor showing and we didn't find out the answer until supper, when we started to eat our rooster. I was served a drumstick and was proceeding to take myself a bite of very expensive chicken when I almost broke my bridgework. I have never seen such a tough piece of meat in all my life…

I am eternally indebted to my grandmother for culling such an array of ancestral history, and for providing fodder to create mixed-media pieces of artwork that will tell the stories of my family tree more visually.

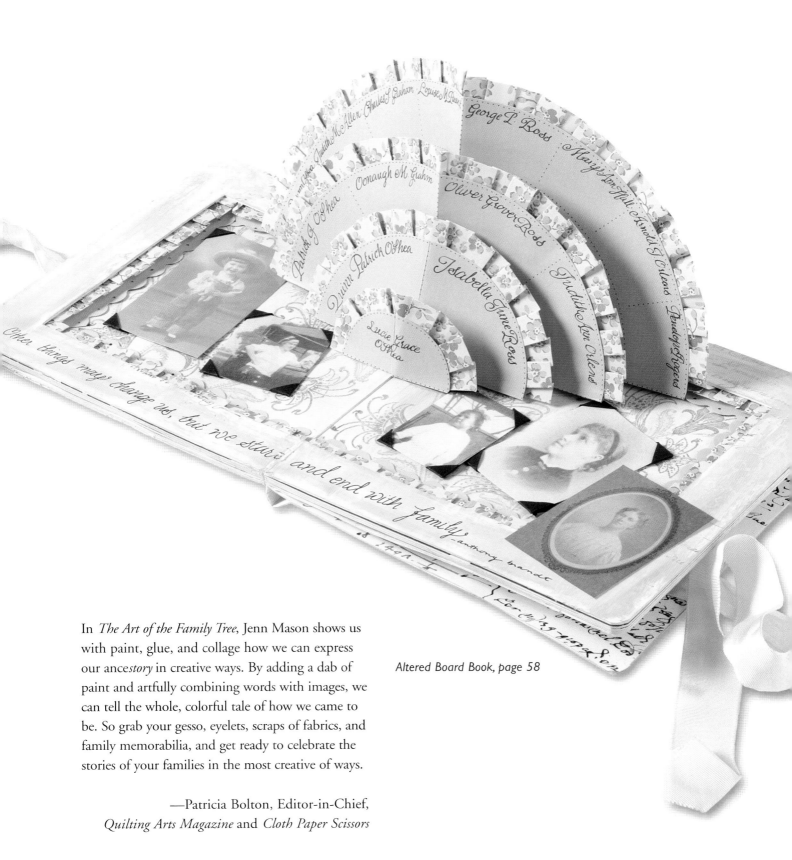

Altered Board Book, page 58

In *The Art of the Family Tree*, Jenn Mason shows us with paint, glue, and collage how we can express our ance*story* in creative ways. By adding a dab of paint and artfully combining words with images, we can tell the whole, colorful tale of how we came to be. So grab your gesso, eyelets, scraps of fabrics, and family memorabilia, and get ready to celebrate the stories of your families in the most creative of ways.

—Patricia Bolton, Editor-in-Chief,
Quilting Arts Magazine and *Cloth Paper Scissors*

Introduction

I was destined to write this book. Everything in my life has pointed me to creating the projects in this book to share with you. Grandiose words, I know, but consider the following:

I have a big family. I come from a large Irish-Catholic family that lives within a twenty-mile radius (with me and a couple of others as the exceptions).

My mother made family trees. For some time, my mother made wooden handcrafted family trees she customized during the big craft fair boom. To this day she gets requests from her old customers for their new family members whose names she writes on little wooden hearts and mails back.

I married into a family with a well-researched genealogy. My husband's great-grandfather spent his days in retirement actively researching both his family history and that of his son-in-law. His daughter, my husband's grandmother, dutifully and patiently typed out all of his research into two books. (I can't imagine how much time this must have taken.)

I have current family members interested in family research. My mother-in-law is now the family detective tracing those whom she calls the "lost girls"—a group of family ancestors about whom little is known (yet!). And, my father is working diligently to discover more about his family with the help of his wonderful aunt and an old family bible.

I am an artist.

Those are reasons enough. But your story doesn't have to be like mine to be able to appreciate this book. Every time I told someone about this book I was working on, I would inevitably get to hear their family story. Some people said that their family was too complicated to make into a family tree. Some said that they had too little information or wished that they had more pictures. Others said that they knew five generations on their mother's side of the family but that their father's side was mostly unknown. And then there were a few who just wanted to know more about the projects I was working on.

This book is for all of these people. We all have families even if they are disjointed, adopted, married into, or thrust upon us. How we tell our story is up to us. *The Art of the Family Tree* is here to walk you through your journey. Whether you are a prolific artist who is just starting to research your past or an experienced genealogist who has long been frustrated over the lack of ideas for turning your research into a family showcase, this book has something for you. Among the projects are solutions such as **It's All Relatives** (page 82), which helps to document the family ancestry when not every member of the branches are known, **The Women Who Made the Men** (page 48), which follows a single line of ancestral descent, and **Hiding Jacob's Ladder** (page 66), which honors one generation of grandchildren.

The projects in the book are divided into three chapters—wall art, book art, and three-dimensional art. Each project is accompanied by **Ance*story*** (page 24) and **Finding Inspiration** sections that will help to guide and inspire both genealogists and artists alike. If you desire further inspiration, take in the beautiful projects in the gallery by several talented fabric, collage, mixed-media, and calligraphic artists.

When teaching, I tell my students that I only have two rules. The first is that I would appreciate it if they laughed at my jokes. The second is that I never expect them to make the exact same project that is being taught and that they are free to alter their project as I teach. Throughout this book I have provided little tidbits called **Making It Personal** that will help serve as a guide for customizing your project. As far as laughing at my jokes—well, I'll leave that up to you.

So gather your family bible or that old box of "stuff" from the attic, the pictures left to you by your great-aunt Penny from Pacific Palisades, a notebook and pencil, and let's get started. I hope you enjoy your journey through the past as much as I did!

–Jenn Mason

Getting Started

The most important part of creating art like the pieces in this book is to have a space that makes you feel good to work in and to have tools and materials that you enjoy creating with. If you can't enjoy the process, then the result is much less rewarding.

Finding Space

As an artist I have carved out many different types of spaces to work in, from a drafting table and uncomfortable stool in a guest room/office/storage room, to a giant space in a room above a two-car garage with a long conference table swimming in the middle of it. I dream of one day having a room large enough to house a big easel with plenty of windows overlooking a garden. Until then, I will make do and enjoy the space I'm in.

It is a complete luxury to have a room all to yourself; many people must find alternate spaces. It's important to have some space where supplies are easily accessed and works in progress may be left out. For me, the kitchen table is a dangerous place to work.

If you don't have a space to work in or don't enjoy working in the space you currently use, take a walk through your home and see if you can look at it from a different perspective. Could you remove the doors from a guest room closet and add shelves and a small desk? What about an empty wall in a living or dining room—is there space there for an antique hutch that you might enjoy searching for in antique markets that would fit that space and store your supplies nicely? Could you use a corner of a spare bedroom by keeping your supplies in rolling boxes under the bed?

Organizing Space

Once you have your space, it must be organized in a way that works for you. While it's nice to have neat, organized shelves, you'll probably want to be able to get out and put away your supplies easily. If boxes of materials are all closed up and packed away, you may be less likely to get supplies out to work. My solution? Small white bins without tops that disguise the contents but make cleanup a breeze. What works for you? Do you have a pile of papers you need to have at the ready or a tackle box full of tools? Don't be afraid to rearrange your space until it feels right. I've moved several times, but now setting up my space is a breeze. Once I configure my shelves, I start unpacking my white bins and paper shelves, I set my three pencil carousels on my desk within reach, and I'm eager to get started.

Tools and Materials

One of my first professors in art school gave me my most important piece of advice. When it comes to tools, "buy the best you can afford." I scoffed at first because I was a poor college student putting myself through school, but I heeded his advice and seventeen years later the good pieces I bought still serve me well.

Three of the best ways to find tools and materials you love to work with are to ask other artists, to experiment, and to read getting-started sections like this one. Every artist you talk to will have a different "must-have list" (see the sidebar for the top-five lists from some of the contributing gallery artists, page 15), but there are certain supplies that most of us consider basics. If you're new to the kind of art created in this book, this is my list of necessities. Consider all of these as you build your own collection of basic supplies.

SCISSORS—You'll need fabric, paper, detail, and decorative-edge varieties.

CRAFT KNIFE—Use on a self-healing cutting mat.

BLACK WRITING PENS—Micron pens in multiple sizes work well; the point size 005 allows you to write *very* tiny.

AWL—A handy tool, not just for poking holes.

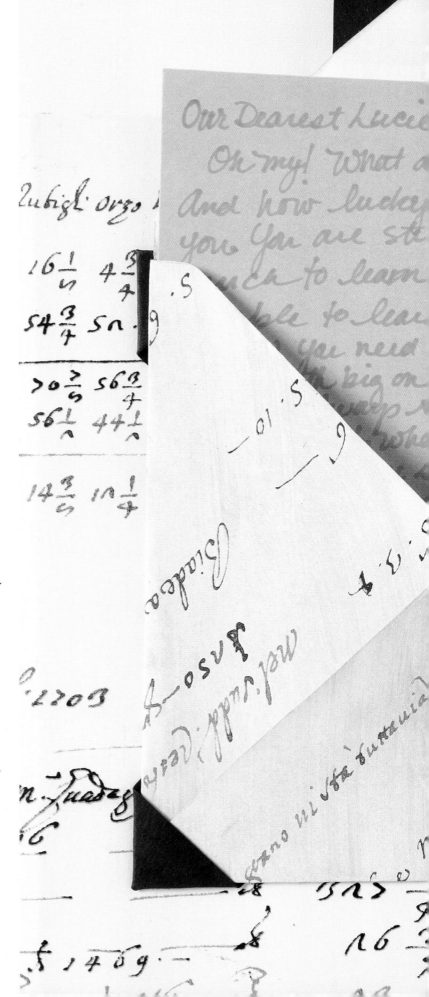

Fig. 1

for getting quick coverage and also a set of synthetic white bristle and watercolor brushes in a variety of sizes for other paint jobs.

PAINTS, MEDIUMS, AND GROUNDS—There are many glazes, fluid acrylics, and gel mediums and acrylic paints available. (I mostly use those made by Golden.)

Filling in the Gaps

The previous list includes must-haves but seek out other treasures to work with. Trips to antique stores, flea markets, and garage sales are great sources for collage material. Here are some items to watch for:

OLD BOOKS—especially those with interesting subjects, illustrations, or engravings that can work into a project. Look for books from before the 1920s so that you don't abuse any copyrights. A great find is always a giant old dictionary (Fig. 1).

OLD PAPERS—especially old letters, cards, correspondences, and ledgers. This photograph shows canceled checks from the 1920s, an old pharmacist's prescription book, and a general store ledger. Postage stamps also lend a feeling of history (Fig. 2).

UNIQUE OBJECTS—especially items that can be altered or added to a piece of art. Look for old bottles, musical instruments, cigar boxes, and ceramic photographic supply letters (Fig. 3).

Other fun items that you may want to consider are eyelets, tags, and shrink-plastic embellishments. Brass charms and other metallic doodads can add a little sparkle, as can the occasional touch of

PENCILS—Try mechanical pencils, and white erasers are a must.

ADHESIVES—3M and Xyron products are quite reliable, and choose a good archival glue for bookbinding-type projects.

HOLE PUNCHES—$\frac{1}{16}$" (1.6 mm), $\frac{1}{8}$" (3 mm), and $\frac{1}{4}$" (6 mm) are most frequently used.

RULER—18" (45.7 cm) metal ruler with a cork backing and a 36" (91.4 cm) metal ruler for tearing big sheets of watercolor paper for deckle-edged pages.

BONE FOLDER—Use this for folding and scoring.

PAINTBRUSHES—Use cheap foam ones

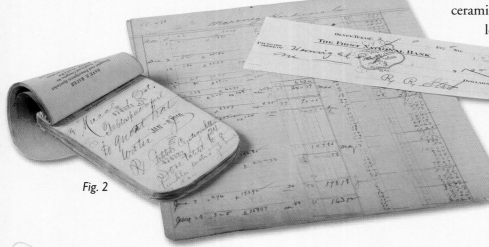

Fig. 2

Contributing Artists' Top-Five Favorite Materials List

It was hard for the artists to pick just a few of the "must-haves" in their work space. This is their list of items other than the essentials (scissors, paper trimmer, craft knife, bone folder, etc.).

Velvet, cool stencils with dye-based sprays, gold stick-on square metal studs, Schmincke metallic dry gouache powder (sprinkled in my paint pots and then written with my dip pens), and smooth muslin.
— Lisa Engelbrecht

Pencil (I use one in every piece), found images, pushpins (I use them to mock up stuff), soft rags, and my hands.
— Lynn Whipple

One of my favorite art supplies is a small sponge sander (I buy it at Ace Hardware)—I sand all of my surfaces to give them an aged look.
— Janice Lowry

Fluid acrylics, fabric, Lutradur, Sakura Micron Pigma pen, and Photoshop.
— Lesley Riley

I can't work without tweezers, Tim Holtz Distress Ink pads (especially Vintage Photo), and trims (like the vine trim I used on my gallery piece.)
— Anita Byers

Old ledger papers, antique natural history egg exemplars from my father's egg farm, little grassy nests, real quail and dove eggs (like the ones dad raised), and found materials from my garden such as feathers, twigs, lichen, palm fiber, and the spent leaves from my spring daffodils.
— Catherine Moore

Sponge dauber and ink, crystals, great adhesive, Krylon leafing pens, and little accessories.
— Michelle Bodensteiner

glitter (German glass glitter is a favorite). Beads, wire, and jump rings can come in handy, as can cardboard letter stencils and waxed linen thread. Waterslide decals called Lazertran are delightful, and don't forget any of the hundreds of rubber stamps and inks that are easily available. Oh, and did I mention ribbon?

As you can see, this list could go on forever. I enjoy the challenge of using a new embellishment or reinterpreting an old standby. As you read through the projects you may be introduced to new tools and materials that you haven't used before. Browse the Resources section at the back of the book (page 129) for ideas on where to find some of these specific items. Feel free to change things up with your own collections and keepsakes to create something all about you and your magnificent family. Most of all, enjoy the process.

Fig. 3

Chapter One
PLANTING YOUR FAMILY TREE

Top Down and Bottoms Up!, page 18

Using What You Have, page 20

Although it may be tempting to skip straight to the art, this chapter explains many of the details involved in making family trees. The sections are informative and concise and should answer many of your initial questions. And be sure to read the final chapter, A Beginner's Guide to Researching Family History, page 108.

In **Top Down and Bottoms Up!**, examples are provided to explain precisely what differentiates one type of family tree from another.

Using What You Have helps you make sense of and organize the information, photographs, and supplies you already have. This section is especially helpful with ideas for combining new and old photographs, for filling in the blanks on

Solving Tricky Family Dilemmas, page 22

Telling Your Ancestory, page 24

incomplete family trees, and for finding interesting ways to use family memorabilia.

If you need suggestions on how to deal with divorce, adoption, or remarriages, read **Solving Tricky Family Dilemmas**.

Learn more about how to incorporate more than just names, dates, or pictures into a family tree in **Telling Your Ance*story***.

And, for those who wander through the flea markets in search of old photographs of other people's families, there is **Adopting Ancestors**.

With this information under your belt, you will be well positioned to create your very own fabulous family tree.

Top Down and Bottoms Up!

GETTING ORIENTED MAY BE the most challenging part of turning pages of family research into a cohesive network of family names and dates. Many of the decisions on how to proceed are personal preference. Whether the desired outcome is to highlight a direct line of descent, a maternal or paternal bloodline, a small generational tree, or a full-out ten-generation family tree, the best way to begin is by sketching out the names in a loose tree chart to get a feeling for the amount of space or layout requirements. Before starting, you'll need to determine if you want to create a top-down or bottoms-up tree. Let's explore these two styles along with a few other alternatives.

Bottoms-up family tree

Top-down

Also known as a descendent-style or drop-line family tree, the top-down style starts with a target person or married couple and follows their descendents. This would include their children, their children's spouses, their grandchildren and their spouses, and their great-grandchildren and their spouses for as many generations as desired.

Top-down family tree

Think of a top-down chart as a great way to commemorate the lives of a family built by one specific ancestor (or a couple). This type of tree makes a perfect gift for a grandparent—just remember to update the tree as new grandchildren and great-grandchildren arrive.

Bottoms-up

This type of tree is also called an ancestor, or pedigree, tree. To create a bottoms-up style tree, start with one target person and trace him back through his parents and their parents' parents for as many generations as possible. This style excludes siblings on all levels.

Think of a bottoms-up chart as a sort of "where did I come from?" map. This type of tree makes an ideal wedding gift. Starting with the new couple as the target "person," the tree can follow the ancestors backward and, upon the arrival of the couple's first child, names can be added among the "roots" of the tree.

Alternate Tree Styles

There are a few other charts and tree styles worth

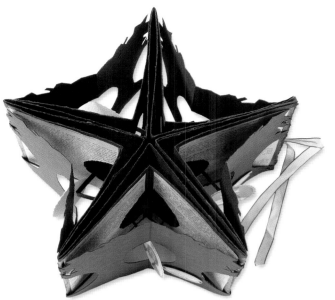

Direct-line family tree

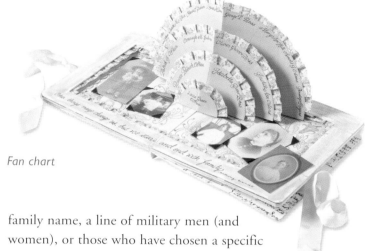

Fan chart

discussing here. These include a fan chart, a circle chart, direct line, and unstructured trees.

Fan Chart

A fan chart is aptly named because of its shape. Starting in the center and radiating out like spokes of a wheel, the fan chart is a more structured way of recording a family lineage. Also consider using the blank chart (page 124) as an overlay on a collage.

Circle Chart

Again named for its shape, the circle chart lends an interesting layout structure to what would normally just be lines and lines of names. In a way, the circle chart engages the viewer to interact with it by the need to turn to read names and dates.

Direct Line

A direct-line style of family tree changes the focus from one multigenerational tree to one specific defining trait throughout many generations. This trait could be a line of men who share the same

Unstructured family tree

family name, a line of military men (and women), or those who have chosen a specific profession such as a line of farmers or teachers in the family.

Unstructured Trees

This is the free spirit of the family tree categories. An unstructured tree is really more a collection of family information than a graphical chart. This style is perfect for those who are just starting to collect family history or for those who have more holes than they do information.

Circle chart

Using What You Have

THERE IS NO BETTER place to start than with what you currently have. Gather it all in one place—all the photographs, dates, family bibles, written histories, old letters, anything that will help you to honor your family tree. If you wish to find more information than you already have, there are many great places to look. Start with relatives and then delve further. Chapter 6 provides several ideas on how to get started researching and includes lists of helpful websites, magazines, and books. Let's talk about some of the other items you might like to use in your projects.

Photographs on this piece were all scanned and printed in the same tones even though they came from the 1930s through current times. (See page 34.)

touched up with software or by a company offering photography restoration services.

If you are trying to incorporate photographs from several eras, it is usually easiest to convert them all to the same color. Since you can't turn black-and-white photographs into color, it is best to turn the color photographs into black and white.

You may also have a collection of photographs of family members at different ages and may be unsure about which ones to use. This is a matter of personal preference, as are many issues in the design of the family tree. It may be fun to consider making a family tree with all childhood photographs to show the resemblances between the family members.

Photographs

If you have photographs of many generations, they are all going to look very different. Cabinet card photographs (or if you're lucky, tin types) will be old, possibly faded, and black and white or sepia. They may also be damaged, torn, dirty, or cracked. Many of these problems can be corrected with easy-to-use software or by specialty photography stores.

Pictures from the era of new color photographs may be discolored or faded. Again, these can be

Mossy Mementos offers a glimpse in to a family of siblings as infants. Beautiful white apparel and wide eyes make for an interesting family collection. (See page 86.)

This tree is missing photographs for the four children who died as babies or young children. Each child is represented by a brass dove and a heart in place of his or her photograph. (See page 62.)

Photographs don't have to be used in a family tree at all. Many of the projects in this book with photographs could easily be altered to only include names and dates of family members. If the problem is not having everyone's photograph to fill a tree, try finding a substitute for the missing photographs such as a silhouette (there are clip art books filled with these) or a small icon.

Names and Dates

Names and dates are the standard information collected by genealogists, but it isn't always easy to find everybody's information. Basic information may include the following:

Name
Date of Birth
Place of Birth
Date of Baptism
Place of Baptism
Date of Marriage
Place of Marriage
Spouse's Name
Children's Names
Occupation
Date of Death
Place of Death (and/or Burial)

As you can see, that's a lot of information to place on a piece of art! Spend some time deciding what you want your family tree to communicate. Do you want those who see your tree to know the names of the family members, when family members were married, what kind of professions your ancestors held, or where your family members lived? These questions will help you sort through the information and help you plan out the space on your art piece.

Old Letters, Books, and Keepsakes

Is there an author in the family or a letter writer from the days pre-dating emails? Pages in books, old letters, and family keepsakes such as recipes and ticket stubs can all be tucked into or added on to a project. If the project doesn't lend itself to a specific piece of memorabilia, consider adding a pocket to the back of the piece, if possible, to hold the item close to the tree for the benefit of future generations.

If you're determined to write down all the information listed above, this project (on page 54) will help you to collect the information and dates in an artistic way.

Solving Tricky Family Dilemmas

THERE ARE MANY FAMILY "situations" that can cause some distress while creating a family tree. As we talk about these different issues, including divorce, remarriage, and adoption, the most important thing to keep in mind is making your target audience happy—even if that happens to be you.

Divorce and Multiple Spouses

When dealing with how to handle a divorce on a family tree, first consider the final outcome of the project. If there were no children from the divorce, it may be easy to choose to leave off the divorced spouse. If there are children, however, removing a parent may cause undue tension. Remember that the children are half of each parent regardless of who is raising them.

In terms of how a divorced couple is going to appear on the tree, consider using placement or embellishment as a tool for differentiating that couple from the married couples (below). This becomes especially important when there is a remarriage. There are also easy ways of adjusting the projects

By changing the placement of the dividing flowers, additional spouses can easily be added to the rings of this tree.

to include additional spouses, who joined the family due to divorce or loss of a spouse. This may be especially pertinent to earlier generations who may have had a tendency to remarry two or more times due to loss of a spouse to illness, wartime, or accidents. Trees such as Quilted Memories (above) and Family Orchard (opposite, bottom) can be altered to accommodate these additions.

If you're attempting to create a bottoms-up, ancestor-style family tree, it may actually make more sense to include the spouse that the following generation came from instead of the remarriage. Again, this will depend on who the tree is ultimately for and the actual family dynamics involved. When laying out a family tree, the man (or husband) is usually on the left and the woman (or wife) on the right. When you're adjusting a

On this tree, the divorced couple is subtly placed farther apart than the married couples, offering a considerate but not glaring solution.

tree to fit a second or third spouse, consider the placement of the children—especially when children are born or added from multiple parents.

Adoption

Another sensitive topic when considering family trees is how to handle adoptions. This manifests itself in many ways. For the die-hard genealogist, it may be imperative that the bloodline is truly mapped out. For others who have been touched by adoption there is no separation between those who are related by blood or love.

Very often, especially in previous generations, a family member was adopted by extended family when parents died. This can be a challenge when the child belongs to two families on a tree. Don't be limited by convention. Add the child in both places if you wish or make note of the family he was adopted by. Consider the age of the child when this happened as well.

These days many children have "open" adoptions where the information of their birth parents is known, but in the past, adoptions were often more secretive, with children sometimes not even knowing that they were adopted. Use your best judgment; a family tree is meant to honor a family in whatever form it comes in, not to cause tension and distrust.

The other issue affecting adopted children is which family tree to trace. For grown adoptees, discovering who they are and where they came from is never far from their thoughts. If they are able to locate their birth family and would like a way to showcase it, a family tree project like any of those in this book can be a wonderful form of art therapy or a project in which they can interact with their birth family. The adoptive family is not to be forgotten; in fact, it is quite possible for the adoptee to document both the nurture and nature sides of her family tree.

In any of the ancestral trees in this book, a subject starts at the bottom of the tree and is then split with the father on the left and the mother on the right. Adoptees can place themselves as the subject of the tree and have birth parents on one side of the tree and adoptive parents on the other side, then continue back from there.

Regardless of the family situation, there is a tree with a solution that can document, honor, and display all the members of the family. Keep in mind your intended audience, then approach the challenges with sensitivity and kindness.

The addition of circles can add a spouse on this tree. With plenty of space in which to write the wedding dates, this tree can be easily adjusted.

Telling Your Ancestory

WHEN CREATING A FAMILY TREE, a story is told by who you choose to show (ancestors, descendents, and so on) and how you choose to present it artistically.

But the story doesn't have to end there. These days many people are recording their family histories and even putting the information they have gathered into book form. For others, only small tidbits of information are known but they don't have a good way of documenting this information. Telling your ance*story* is a way to do just that.

As you work on these projects you may find out interesting anecdotes about the subjects of the tree or come upon old letters or notes jotted down on the backs of photographs. These stories should be recorded and, if possible, added to the tree you are working on.

An ance*story* can take many forms:

STORIES—collected from living relatives or previously told by earlier generations (opposite, top left)

POEMS—written especially for a project or recorded earlier (opposite, top right)

LETTERS—jotted down and tucked inside a project for the recipient to later discover (opposite, bottom left)

FACTS—extra dates, places, and documentation (below)

QUOTATIONS—show the feeling or intent with wise (and sometimes humorous) words about families and relationships (opposite, bottom right)

How you choose to include an ance*story* can be an integral part of your design. In this book many different ideas are presented. Each project has its own ance*story* to serve as an example. The stories are then tucked in, written on the back, worked in to the design, or surround the design. Taking the time to document the histories, stories, and feelings now will be a gift to future generations.

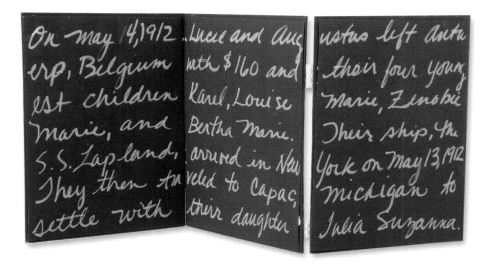

Adopting Ancestors

WHEN ARTISTS CREATE ART, the process is quite often all-consuming. If they are painting a picture, they might think of who has looked upon this scene before. They may wonder how to translate the feeling of the sun shining on their shoulders, or how what they paint on this canvas will affect the viewer. They are actually telling a story; each stroke of the paintbrush is another sentence, paragraph, or chapter. When we create, especially with the projects in the book, we tell a story as well. As a purely creative exercise, remember that your story does not necessarily have to be true! Just as the painter may choose to paint the sky green and the grass orange, we too can make up stories with our paper and paste, photographs, and fabric.

When you happen upon a box of old photographs of stiffly posed people from the turn of the century, you may be immediately intrigued.

Consider telling a story of an unknown family of "adopted ancestors" with your talents. Engage the viewer, add to the questions, make a statement.

Where did this child come from? Why was his picture taken? Did this soldier survive the war? Was this woman loved by a husband? How many grandchildren did this couple have? You may desire to sharpen the story and discover the truths, as though they are portrayed in an out-of-focus picture. But alas, often the stories are lost to time. That is, until we come along and rewrite them. How easily we can marry one woman to a dapper soldier and give them children from this box of photographs. How easily we can give them a story. Our project then becomes like that of the painter or the creative writer—a story of imagination.

Consider telling a story of an unknown family of "adopted ancestors" with your talents. Engage the viewer, add to the questions, make a statement. All it takes is a leap of faith and a sense of curiosity.

Chapter Two
ESPALIER TREES: Art for the Wall

Branching Out, page 30

A Layered Family, page 34

The French word *espalier* is a horticultural term referring to a tree or shrub that has been trained to grow in a flat plane against a wall or trellis. We use it here to describe family trees that are designed similarly, as flat artwork for the wall. Probably the most expected type of family tree art falls in to this category, though I hope this chapter will have you looking at new and beautiful ways to present and enjoy such family trees. In addition, you will find charts in different styles that you can use for these projects starting on page 114.

In **Branching Out**, gesso-covered curly willow branches were grafted together to make a specimen-style family tree. Housed in a shadowbox, this project is the essence of sophistication. A simple variation in a smaller size uses flags instead of leaves to create a family tree perfect for a child's room.

A Layered Family is a happy collage with a whimsical edge. Although it looks difficult, all the elements have been supplied for you to copy and paste. If you're a seasoned artist, read the Making It Your Own section for instructions on how to create your own collage. The miniature variation collage is a perfect example of the possibilities achieved by changing scale.

Family Orchard, page 38

Quilted Memories, page 42

Family Orchard, like **A Layered Family**, has a watercolor tree all ready for you to copy and decorate. Again, if you choose, there are details to personalize in the Making It Your Own section. The variation for this project is a lesson in mono-tone. Photocopying in black and white instead of color gives the family tree a vintage feel.

Quilted Memories provides a soft family tree in a fabric collage. Bits of millinery flowers or other memorabilia can be used to personalize your piece. This tree can also be adjusted easily to add additional spouses. A quick lesson in painting on canvas, including image transfers, may inspire other ideas too.

Creating a tree for the wall may be the most expected type of family tree, but it certainly doesn't have to be boring. These projects inject life into what is traditionally a static, two-dimensional art form. Each one is a showpiece of family heritage. Whether you employ sticks, collage, watercolors, or fabric in to your art for the wall, the outcome will be one of personal vision and unexpected delight.

Branching Out:
Shadowboxed Tree

Materials

- shadowbox frame
- curly willow branches (look for interesting branches with y-shaped formations)
- deerskin or leather lace
- card stock
- small tags
- label (see clip art, page 125)
- double-stick tape
- gesso
- $\frac{1}{16}$" (1.6 mm) eyelets
- waxed linen thread
- hot glue or other three-dimensional adhesive
- black writing marker
- jump rings

Tools

- shrub pruner
- paintbrush
- $\frac{1}{16}$" (1.6 mm) hole punch
- decorative-edge scissors
- needle-nose pliers

A FAMILY TREE MADE from a tree? This piece is just such a tree, complete with grafted branches. This tree is easily extended or pruned to fit your subject family, and it is beautiful in its simplicity. The tree branches are curly willow that are available from florists and import stores but could just as easily come from more sentimental locations, such as a tree in your backyard or from a family's vacation home or old farm. The leaves on this tree are simple shapes cut with decorative-edge scissors. For variety, trace oak, maple, or ginkgo (great for a Chinese ancestry) leaves, or use die-cut leaves. Shadowboxes are easy to find in a number of styles to accommodate trees of any size. The organic form lends itself to grafting on additional branches for families with challenging configurations, such as second marriages.

Instructions

1. Draw a sketch of what type of tree and branches you'll need for your particular family.

2. Choose branches that follow this shape as closely as possible, looking for y-shaped branches. The fewer the "grafted" branches, the easier it is to construct.

3. Apply gesso to all of the branches and let dry (Fig. 1).

4. Lay out the branches following the sketch created in step 1. Use double-stick tape to secure "grafted" branches together. Next, carefully wrap over the tape with the deerskin lace to finish the graft, making sure to tuck in the ends (Fig. 2).

5. Cut leaves out of card stock with decorative-edge scissors and write all the pertinent information on them with the black marker.

6. Punch two holes in the end of each leaf and tie onto the branches with waxed linen thread. Write the wedding dates on the small tags and add eyelets and jump rings. Tie the tags to the branches by looping waxed linen thread through the jump ring (Fig. 3).

7. Fill out the clip art label and insert into the shadowbox.

8. Use hot glue or three-dimensional adhesive to attach the tree to the shadowbox. (The shadowbox shown had a fabric background. If your shadowbox does not have a fabric background you can use spray adhesive and your choice of fabric to customize it.)

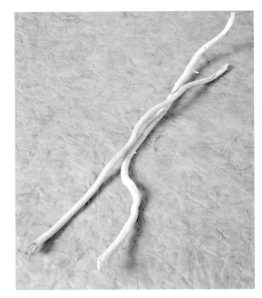

Fig. 1

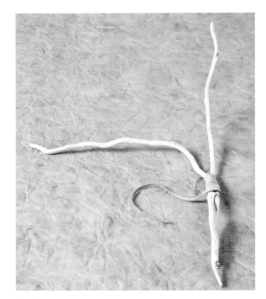

Fig. 2

Fig. 3

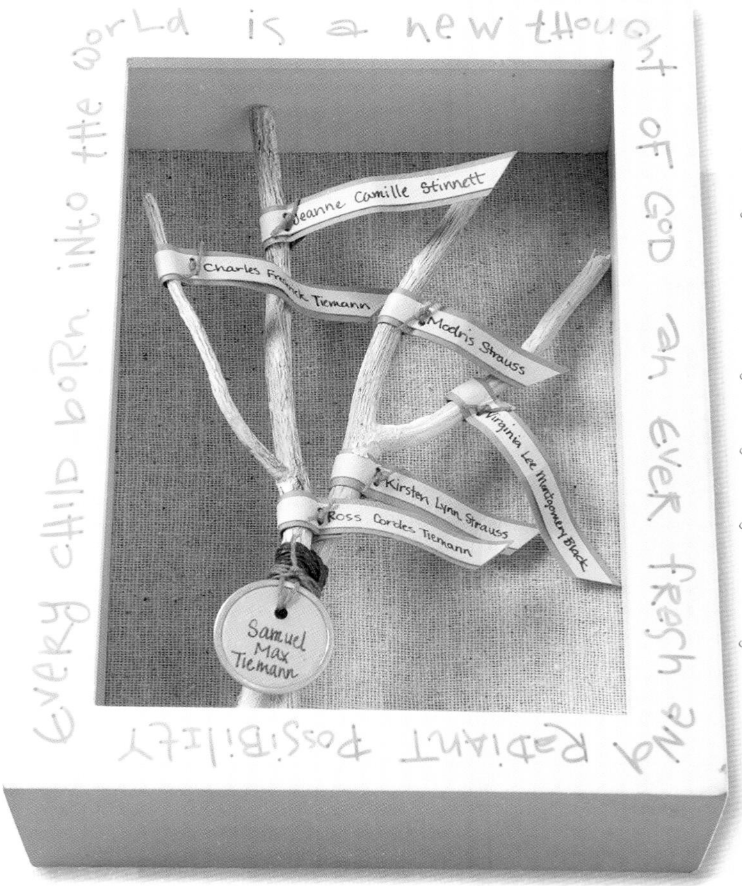
every child born into the world is a new thought of God an ever fresh and Radiant Possibility
Jeanne Camille Stinnett
Modris Strauss
Virginia Lee Montgomery Black
Kirsten Lynn Strauss
Ross Cordes Tiemann
Samuel Max Tiemann

Variation IDEAS

- *Try using different shapes, such as the flags used on this mini tree made for a little boy's room.*
- *Change the colors.*
- *Use different leaf shapes.*
- *Try different papers, such as thin sheet metal or vellum, for interesting leaves.*
- *Try a descendent tree instead by starting at the top and going down.* *(See Watercolor Tree project, page 38.)*

Finding Inspiration

It seems only natural to include an actual tree in a project within this book. I decided to use some curly willow branches but felt that they would be more striking if they were all gessoed to a stark white. Because of my love of gardening I was intrigued by the idea of "grafting" branches. The deerskin laces are thin and flat and easy to wrap around and can be found at large craft stores. I tried to find an interesting way to label the marriages and came up with little tags, jump rings, and one of my favorite paper art elements—$\frac{1}{16}$" (1.6 mm) mini eyelets. I also adore old specimen labels and fashioned this one to be reminiscent of some old favorites.

Ance*story*

Polly and John's story had an icy start. Not how you might expect a love story to begin. You could say that Polly was John's "ice princess"—meant in the nicest of ways, of course. The two met on an ice skating rink while practicing for an ice-dancing recital. John was in high demand as one of the few available men in the skating troupe. We're not sure if Polly was smitten by John's smooth skating or if he won her heart over a mug of hot cocoa but we do know that they were married by October that year. They went on to have three children, five grandchildren and, at last count, four great-grandchildren.

A LAYERED FAMILY:
Collaged Canvas

Materials

- color copy (or scan) of collage, tree, house, and cameos (page 114)
- canvas of desired size and depth
- soft gel matte medium
- foam adhesive squares or tape
- black writing marker
- black-and-white photographs
- glue stick

Tools

- decorative-edge scissors
- craft knife
- cutting mat
- disposable foam brush
- detail scissors

THE DETAIL ON THIS COLLAGE is part of its charm. The bright colors and whimsical cameos make this a piece to lighten up the stodgiest of rooms. By printing all the photographs in black and white the project quickly becomes a cohesive piece of art. The project uses a photocopy of a prepainted collage background, a tree, a house, and a set of cameos; however, you can easily alter any of these elements and create your own (see the sidebar on page 37). Choose a thick canvas for a gallery-like piece or adhere your tree to a flat canvas board and frame it with a mat—either way it will be a one-of-a-kind conversation piece.

INSTRUCTIONS

1. Cut a color photocopy of the background to fit the canvas. If using a canvas larger than the copy size, use one or more extra copies to extend the collage.

2. Quickly cover the canvas with the gel medium and the back of the collage using a foam brush. Adhere the collage to the canvas, smooth out any air bubbles, and coat with another layer of the gel medium.

3. Cut out the tree and house, and use the gel medium to attach them to the collage in the same manner. Let dry.

4. Use the black writing marker to loosely trace around the tree and house form.

from top to bottom: John William Mass III (Preston) b. 9 feb 1911 d. 13 jan 2002 Robert Noble b. 23 Aug 1914 1987. Robert Louis Talbot b. 21 March 1918 d. 5 Dec 1917. Ernest Sheldon b. 13 Jan 1920 d. 27 Oct 2003 Dorothy John Wallace (Jack) Mason d. 13 April 1974 Robert Michael Talbot 9 Oct 1946. Lucy Jean Sheldon 29 July 1949. Matthew Noble Mason b. 1 Aug 1971 Jennifer Lynn Talbot 29 June 1971. Abigail Dorothy-Rose Mason b. 10 March 2001 Rebecca Louise Mason b. 20 Oct 1999 He that raises a large family does, indeed, while he lives to observe them, stand a broader mark for sorrow; but then he stands a broader mark for pleasure too. Benjamin Franklin

b 26 May 1914 d. 18 dec 1976 Louise Mass millicent Kyle b. 9 July 1919 d. 27 mar 1995 muriel Jensen Beck 18 April 1919 d. 21 Sept 1981 Margaret Smith b. 29 sept 1923 d. 10 Jan 2004 millicent Noble b. 3 Sept 1945.

Fig. 1 Have fun with your journaling—list all the names of the people in the photographs or tell your story.

5. Cut out the photos in silhouette and place on foam dots on the cutout cameo shape.

6. Use a glue stick or other adhesive to attach the cameos to the background.

7. Use the black marker to journal along the bottom part of the landscape (Fig. 1).

Ances*tory*

Rebecca and Abigail Mason are like twin sisters who started out seventeen months apart but grow more and more alike with each passing day. Both girls have curly blonde hair that often becomes the topic of conversation at neighborhood and other friendly gatherings. It seems that no other family on this tree has produced two curly headed children. Their mother has been questioned on more than one occasion if the milkman was a "little too friendly." But no, these two girls were just blessed to have curly hair and the personality to match. Somehow, this tree of parents, grandparents, and great-grandparents managed to pass down the curly-headed gene along with the love of books, art, travel, foreign language, and nature.

Finding Inspiration

In trying to come up with unique family tree ideas, I incorporated some of the techniques that I've been using in some of my other fine art work. The joy of getting paint under my fingernails has fueled a passion for putting paint on canvas in unorthodox ways. Here, I used a faux bois tool because I just happened to find it sitting on my studio shelf. Although the initial coverage was incomplete and streaky, it led me to add a layer, and then another layer, and then a horizon line. I was hooked. After working for a while in this way, it was just a natural progression to create a collage for this book. I try to keep a sense of whimsy in my work. Sometimes it's present in the colors, or the design, or the use of interesting ephemera. Sometimes it's just a little joke that only I will get, but it makes me happy to know it's in there.

Variation IDEAS

- Try enlarging or reducing the collage to vary the size.

- Use paper punches to create different shaped cameos.

- Use names and dates in place of photographs.

- Adjust the placement of the cameos to add or subtract generations.

- Make a descendent tree by starting with one couple at the top of the tree and working down. (See Watercolor Tree project, page 38.)

Making It Your Own

Everything but the photographs is supplied to make this project, but if you're feeling adventurous, try creating your own background and collage elements following these steps.

Creating a Collage Background

Suggested Materials:

- *heavyweight art or watercolor paper, canvas board, or a stretched canvas*
- *paints, glazes, dye-based inks, alcohol inks, fluid acrylics, acrylics, and textile paints*
- *comb tool, sponges, faux bois tool (for making faux wood grain), brushes, paper towels, scrap paper, ephemera to add to the collage, including book pages, sheet music, or old letters*
- *soft gel, gel medium, or other collage adhesive*

1. Paint a semitransparent base coat over the entire canvas or paper. Try using a paint comb or faux bois tool next. Don't worry about covering every last bit of surface; the more layers that are added, the more complexity shows in the end piece.

2. Add pieces of paper ephemera and more layers of paint to blend the painting together. Let some of the layers dry before adding new layers.

3. Use the inks by dripping them on in random areas.

4. Add paint in areas and then lay paper towel or scrap paper over the wet paint to pick up some of the paint. Lay the wet scrap paper over another area of the collage to transfer some of the paint to different areas. This will help unify the overall effect.

5. If the painting seems too wild, try using a thin coat of a white or off-white glaze.

6. Let the entire collage dry thoroughly before using it for your project.

Creating the Tree and House

Suggested Materials:

- *paper ephemera (color copies work wonderfully), dye-based inks*

1. Sketch out your design on the back of the ephemera or copy and cut out.

2. To finish the house, cut out small stamps to create windows and doors.

3. To finish the tree, lay it faceup on scrap paper to protect your work surface and rub it with a brown ink pad to give the tree warmth and dimension.

Creating the Cameos

Suggested Materials:

- *watercolor or other heavyweight paper*
- *paints, glazes, dye-based inks, alcohol inks, fluid acrylics, acrylics, textile paints, and ink pads*
- *sponges, paintbrushes, paper towels, scrap paper, and stamps*
- *oval punches, templates, or die cuts*
- *plain and decorative-edge scissors*
- *paper ephemera such as old ledger paper (color copies will work also)*
- *black writing marker*

1. Create base papers for the bottom two layers of the cameo by painting and inking the heavyweight paper. Let dry.

2. Punch or cut the two back ovals out of the painted and stamped paper.

3. Cut out the top oval from the paper ephemera and outline it roughly with the black marker.

FAMILY ORCHARD:
Watercolor Tree

Materials
- color copy or scan of tree (page 117)
- frame (mat is optional)
- ribbon
- card stock
- foam tape
- computer-generated text or writing implements

Tools
- circle punches, templates, or dies
- scissors

A SOFT WATERCOLOR TREE is the perfect canvas for any family tree. The painting in the Templates and Clip Art section on page 117 makes this project approachable by anyone from a budding family historian to an experienced genealogist. If you have elegant parochial school handwriting or a fine draftsman style of printing, try hand lettering your family circles. Because the names are added individually (or in pairs) to the tree, it's easy to fix a misspelled or imperfect writing attempt. If handwriting is not your forte, the computer is a wonderful substitute with the thousands of different typefaces available online. The tree in this project is a descendent-style tree but it could easily be flipped to be an ancestor tree (page 18).

INSTRUCTIONS

1. Use a computer or writing implement to write the names and dates on card stock.

2. Punch circles out of the printed card stock, layer with foam adhesive tape, and secure to the color copy.

3. Tie the ribbon into bows and trim with scissors. Add the ribbons to the assemblage.

Making It Your Own

If making your own tree appeals to you, these steps will guide you through the relatively simple—and rather therapeutic—process.

Suggested Materials:

- *heavyweight watercolor paper or watercolor canvas board, watercolor pencils or watercolor paints, pencil and eraser, watercolor brushes, water, scrap paper, graphite paper*

1. Start by sketching out the tree design with pencil on scrap paper. Use graphite paper to transfer the design to the watercolor paper. (If graphite paper isn't available, rub the pencil lead along the back side of the drawing before tracing over the sketch.)

2. Start coloring in the tree and leaf designs with the watercolor pencils.

3. Painting with watercolors is a process of adding colors. Start with a little color at a time and add more and more layers to create depth. Unlike painting with acrylics, white cannot be added at the end.

4. Use a wet brush to blend the watercolor pencil. Continue to add color until the painting is finished.

5. If you want to remove color from a section of the painting, try painting over it with clean water and then blot it with a paper towel.

Other ways to use watercolor pencils:

- Scribble small circles of color on scrap paper to create a palette of paints. Draw a wet brush across the circle to pick up color.

- Draw a wet brush across the tip of a watercolor pencil lead to pick up color.

- For a very intense color (good for outlining and adding dark shadows), dip the watercolor pencil in to water and draw with the wet colored lead.

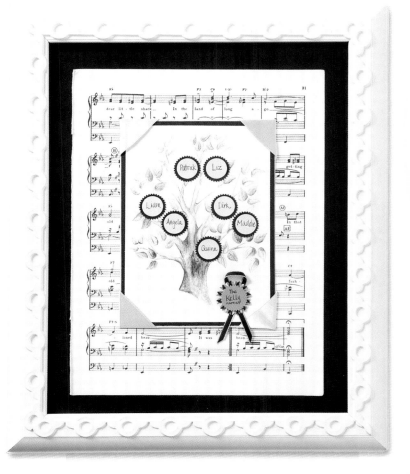

Ancestory

Robert Louis Talbot was a rather quiet man. He survived wartime, owned his own garage, supported his family of five, and outlived his wife Muriel who died in her early sixties after battling cancer. Robert's heart failed him many times, finally requiring him to have bypass surgery, which left him needing a cane. (The cane was beautiful, all covered with souvenir metal shields that provided fond memories of his travels with Muriel.)

Soon after the passing of his wife, Robert had a stroke. The stroke affected his speech and he had to relearn even the simplest of words. It seemed that only when he was truly angry or frustrated would the words clearly flow. Interestingly, the other area of his brain that was affected by the stroke was the part that remembered that he walked with a cane. Even though Robert spent a lot of time working on his speech he never again walked with a cane. He could be found happily playing a quick round of nine holes whenever the weather permitted until the day he died.

Variation IDEAS

- *Try copying the painting on page 117 in black-and-white for a monochromatic family tree.*

- *Flip a tree from a descendent-style tree to an ancestral-style tree.*

- *Use oval, rectangle, or square shapes to add family members to the tree.*

- *Reduce a copy of the tree for a small family tree.*

Finding Inspiration

I wanted to design a dreamy watercolor project that could be transformed easily to fit any family situation. During a sketching session I started to discover the idea of a round, big-leafed tree. The sketches took on a whimsically colorful quality but still had a realistic feel. The final painting was created with watercolor pencils, which I enjoy using for illustrations such as this. See Making It Your Own, opposite, for more information on how to create your own watercolor tree.

Quilted Memories:
Circle Chart Assemblage

Materials

- canvas
- absorbent ground for pastels
- glazing medium
- fluid acrylics
- wool felt
- tacky glue
- paper and millinery flowers
- mat board
- light molding paste
- blending marker or wintergreen oil and cotton ball
- copier or laser printout of family names (with or without dates) in reverse

Tools

- sewing machine or needle and thread
- pinking shears
- bone folder
- palette knife
- sewing pins

IF SEARCHING FOR THE MYSTERY of your family ancestors has you going in circles, then this assemblage is calling your surname. Built on a series of concentric circles hand painted onto canvas and layered with paper and millinery flowers, this piece reinvents the circle family chart. Small sewing details added by hand or with a sewing machine echo ancestral quilts while offering a unique platform for documenting family members. Wool felt is cut with fabric pinking shears to whimsically outline each layer before they are centered on a mat board surface painted with light molding paste and fluid acrylics.

Instructions

1. Mix fluid acrylics with glazing medium and paint onto the canvas with a palette knife to create a variegated background (Fig. 1).

2. When this has dried, use the palette knife to spread a thin layer of absorbent ground over the painted canvas. This will help make an even surface for the image transfers and will keep the canvas from unraveling.

Fig. I

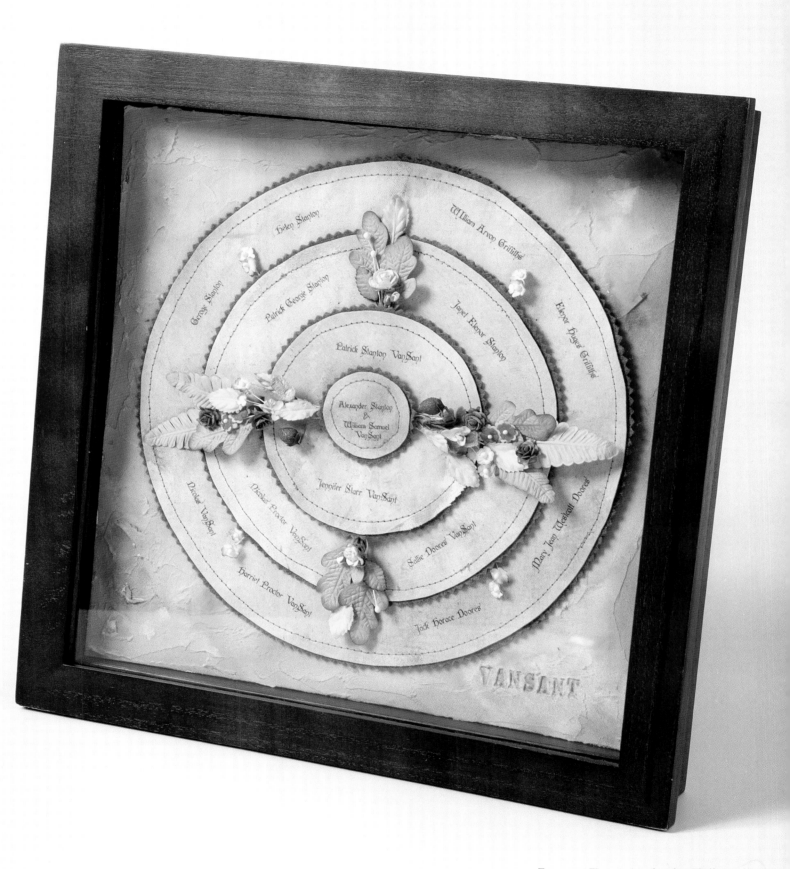

Fig. 2a

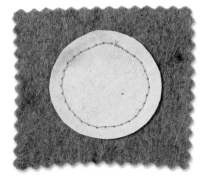

Fig. 2b

Fig. 2c

3. Trace and cut out four concentric circles from the painted canvas (Fig. 2a).

4. Cut a piece of the felt about 1" (2.5 cm) larger than the largest circle and pin the large circle to it right side up (Fig. 2b).

5. Use a sewing machine or hand sew the circles together and then trim the felt with pinking shears. Remove the pins and repeat with the remaining three circles (Fig. 2c).

6. Cut out each of the names and place them facedown over the corresponding spot on the chart. Hold the paper firmly and rub either the cotton ball with wintergreen oil or the blending marker over the back of the paper until it is saturated. Use the bone folder to burnish the paper to the canvas. Carefully pull back the

Fig. 3

paper to reveal the image transfer of the name (and date).

7. Create bunches of flowers to delineate the different family members (Fig. 3).

8. Cut a piece of mat board to fit the frame.

Variation Ideas

⊚ Instead of painting a canvas, try scanning or photocopying the painted background (page 121) onto a piece of printable canvas paper and then add concentric circles.

⊚ Make a small circle chart in a frame without a glass insert.

⊚ Use correction fluid to change a dividing line on the chart to add a future spouse.

Ance*story*

Young Alex and Will are two very lucky boys. They have a large, connected, and emotionally invested family. Their father, Patrick, a part-time volunteer EMT, is capable of fixing or building just about anything, from an entirely gutted kitchen from the 1600s to wooden toys that foster imagination. Jennifer, their mom, is always making them handmade toys and taking them on adventures. Both boys take special pride each summer in tending their own gardens with their mom and happily give tours of their plantings to any visitors showing interest. Aunts, uncles, cousins, and doting grandparents all live nearby, creating a nurturing childhood for the boys—making for two wonderfully engaging young men.

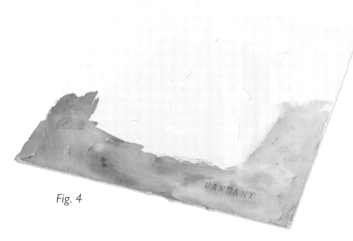

Fig. 4

Cover the mat board with thick coating of light molding paste using a palette knife. (Save on paste by leaving the center of the board blank where the circle tree will go.) (Fig. 4)

9. Use fluid acrylics to color the dried molding paste (Fig. 5).

10. Use the glue to add the flower bunches to the circle and to layer the circles on top of each other in the center of the frame.

Fig. 5

Finding Inspiration

Millinery flowers are sought-after flea market items but aren't always easy to find. And sometimes, when found, the cost is often prohibitive. My solution? Look for old hats to deconstruct. This little green number strewn with white roses and little wild strawberries was a gold mine. The hat itself, in disrepair with its tiny patch of disintegrating netting, sat tucked on a studio shelf as this project came into being. When I decided to create this family tree for this particular family I instantly thought of incorporating the millinery strawberries and other tiny paper flowers to represent the subject's love of nature. From that seed, the project grew.

Making It Personal: Here, millinery flowers and strawberries are used on this family tree to commemorate the family's love of gardens and the outdoors. What could you add to represent your family—old maps, ethnic or regional symbols (flags, colors, or landmarks), or seashells? These items could be used in place of the flowers or in the background.

Chapter Three
LEAFING THROUGH THE YEARS: Book Art

Soft-Sided Memories, page 54

Fanned and Frilly, page 58

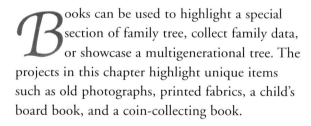

Books can be used to highlight a special section of family tree, collect family data, or showcase a multigenerational tree. The projects in this chapter highlight unique items such as old photographs, printed fabrics, a child's board book, and a coin-collecting book.

The **Women Who Made the Men: Ancestral Star Book** uses a simplified star book form and tree page template (page 128) to create a book showcasing five generations of mothers and daughters-in-law. This book could easily change focus to a family of five or a direct line of descent.

Soft-Sided Memories: Fabric Journal Collection Book is less a formal piece of art than it is what I like to call "everyday art." There's no reason to wait until all the family research is collected to start creating. This book with its soft cover can pack easily into a bag or sit happily next to the computer during an online research surfing trip.

The popping open of **Fanned and Frilly: Altered Board Book** reveals a fan chart decorated in paper ruffles and lace. Made with a child's board book and beautiful papers, paints, and glazes, this project is a great showcase for a family ancestry. The ance*story* in this piece comes in the form of a love letter from three generations to a new family addition.

Framed and Quartered, page 62

Hiding Jacob's Ladder, page 66

Framed and Quartered: Coin Collector's Book is just the piece to commemorate a large family. This project features a farm family from the early 1900s who emigrated from Belgium. All fifteen children and their parents grace this trifold book that is meant to be displayed open.

Hiding Jacob's Ladder: Wooden Book and Shrine could almost fit in to any of the three main chapters of this book. The shrine could be hung on the wall, set on a table, or displayed open like an accordion book. Small photo collages interlaced with wooden pages and stamped, hand-dyed silk ribbon are rested upon four legs and given a place of honor in a matching box.

Library of Relatives: Mini Journals Collections are the perfect venue for recording more information about families of any size. Use a mini journal for one ancestor or an entire family. Simple book-making techniques using ribbon, card stock, and watercolor paper are used to make small books that can be sketched, written, and painted in.

Whether you choose to make one of these projects or a series of them, the process is as rewarding as showing off the finished piece. Remember to include your own Ance*story* (page 24) in your books to share your insights on the family heritage with others. Also consider making a blank book to give as a gift for a fellow family history buff. Enjoy filling your family pages.

THE WOMEN WHO MADE THE MEN:
Ancestral Star Book

Materials

- heavyweight black art paper
- watercolor paper
- vintage book pages
- soft gel
- acrylic glaze
- waxed linen twine
- ribbon
- label holders or die-cut label holders
- ¹⁄₁₆" (1.6 mm) and ⅛" (3 mm) eyelets
- glue stick

Tools

- metal ruler (18" [45.7 cm] or longer)
- eyelet setting tools
- oval paper punches, dies, or templates
- bone folder
- paper towel
- pencil
- foam paintbrush
- paper cutter
- ¼" (6 mm) hole punch
- craft knife and cutting mat
- templates (page 128)
- awl

FOR THOSE WHO HAVE never made a star book before, this project may seem intimidating, but with the exception of accurately measuring a few folds the book goes together rather easily. Long strips of art paper are torn to give the book a more handmade feel and are then overlapped to create even longer strips. This star book has been simplified in its construction and breaks down into three overlapping accordion-folded paper strips, five photos, four stitches, a couple of eyelets, and a ribbon. A star book is meant to be viewed fully open but this book can be "read" traditionally from front to back as well. As in many of the projects with photographs in this book, all of the pictures were converted to black and white. On the back cover I've included a library pocket to include the ance*story* (page 53). This piece makes a great gift that will impress any recipient—but particularly a family member bitten with the genealogy bug.

INSTRUCTIONS

1. Find the grain of the art paper and tear long strips of paper 6" (15.2 cm) wide, short grained. You will need enough strips to make 30", 40", and 45" (76.2, 101.6, and 114.3 cm) strips of paper.

2. To make the first accordion, measure 3" (7.6 cm) intervals along a strip of paper. Score and fold at these intervals. Add multiple folded strips together using a glue stick to create an accordion with five two-page spreads.

3. Repeat step 2 with 4" (10.2 cm) intervals and 4½" (11.4 cm) intervals to create two more accordions.

4. Use the ¼" (6 mm) hole punch to punch a hole halfway down the first and last folds. (This is for the ribbon that will be inserted at the end.)

5. Using the tree template, trace the tree shape onto the smallest accordion and cut out with a craft knife and cutting mat.

6. Cut ten vintage book pages to fit on each panel of the medium accordion and adhere with a half-and-half mixture of soft gel and acrylic glaze (Fig. 1). Brush over the top of each page with this mixture to tint the pages and remove with a paper towel. Let dry.

Fig. 1 By varying the pressure of the towel you can change the amount of glaze on different pages.

7. Using the window template, trace the oval onto the medium accordion and cut out with a craft knife and cutting mat.

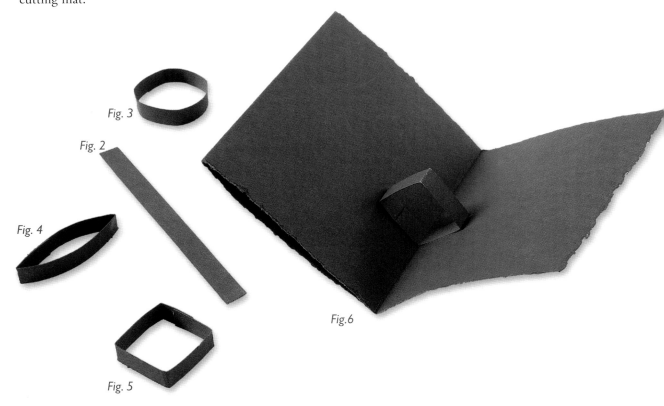

Fig. 3

Fig. 2

Fig. 4

Fig. 5

Fig.6

Making It Personal: *The pages of the vintage book used in this project are hardly readable and yet everyone who previewed the piece asked if there was any significance to the text. Each time I was asked, I was relieved to answer that yes, indeed, I had chosen pages from an old housewives guide to line my book. What could you choose to highlight your subject? Travel essays for a family with wanderlust? An etiquette book from the Victorian era? A French-to-English dictionary representing a foreign ancestry? Try shopping at old bookstores and library book sales looking for unique titles and subject matter—you never know where your next muse may come from.*

Fig. 7

8. Create five pop-up mechanisms for the photographs:
   Cut a strip of paper measuring ½" x 6" (1.3 x 15.2 cm) (Fig. 2).
   Create a loop by overlapping the two ends by ½" (1.3 cm) with a glue stick (Fig. 3).
   Fold the loop flat (Fig. 4).
   Open the loop back up and fold again, making the first two folds touch in the middle, creating a square (Fig. 5).
   Add glue to two sides of the square and adhere to the center fold of a two-page spread. Repeat this step for the remaining pages (Fig. 6).

9. Glaze a piece of watercolor paper in the same way as the book pages in step 6.

10. Punch larger ovals from the watercolor paper and then trim the ovals down with pinking decorative-edge scissors.

11. Use a smaller oval paper punch to cut out photographs and mount them to the bigger, glazed ovals.

12. Put all three accordions together with the largest in the back and the smallest (tree-shaped) one in the front. Use three eyelets to attach the three pieces together along the front edge (Fig. 7).

13. Repeat for the back edge.

14. Using an awl, poke three holes on the front folds where the tree branches intersect (Fig. 8).

15. Use the waxed twine to make a pamphlet stitch (Fig. 9) through these holes and tie in the back.

16. Add die-cut labels or label holders to the pages.

17. From the back of the book, carefully thread the ribbon into the holes in the first and last fold. Pull the ribbons through to the front between the middle and back accordion.

18. If desired, add your ance*story* with a library pocket on the back cover (page 25) and a label on the front cover.

Fig. 8

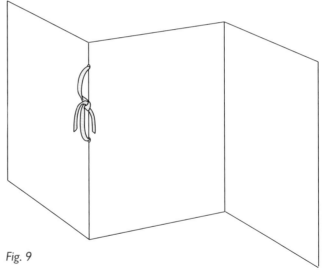

Fig. 9

Making It Personal: This book is about mothers and daughters-in-law quite simply because while I was scanning a relative's archives of old family pictures I realized that I actually had photographs for five genera- tions of in-laws. Who could you commemorate with this book? Fathers and sons-in-law? Military ancestors? Could you do a series of books, each on a different family group?

Ance*story*

I am the youngest member of this book. I am a daughter-in-law and not yet a mother-in-law. Actually, because I have no sons, I am the last chapter of this book. Quite often I think of how fortunate I am to have a wonderful relationship with my mother-in-law. I often like to wonder about how the generations before me got along.

I remember one particular holiday when I was in the kitchen with my soon-to-be mother-in-law preparing the meal. We happened to be discussing just exactly what it was that I should call her after I was married. She said it was perfectly okay to just call her Missy. At about this time in the conversation, Missy's mother-in-law entered into the kitchen to check on the progress of the potato peeling. She just smiled and looked at both of us and said, "I seem to remember having this same conversation some time ago." I'm not positive but I think she winked at me as she turned around and walked out of the kitchen.

Finding Inspiration

Sometimes inspiration comes from something mundane and blossoms into something much more special. In this case, a slew of leftover black-colored art paper from a class I had taught. I knew it tore superbly and that I wanted to create a star book and this piece is the result. The subject of this book was a perfect fit for the five-page spread. Next, I knew that I wanted the story of the book to be told by the reader's interaction with the different photographs. This was simply solved by adding cameos to small simple pop-ups. The final challenge was creating the tree shape. Thanks to having small children in the house, I was quickly able to solve this challenge with my widely revered (at least in my own home) paper doll skills. For some people, working through the paper engineering elements of a project like this may be intimidating, for others exhilarating. Either way, by following instructions for a piece like this and giving it a twist to personalize, each artist has the ability to create a whole new outcome, process, or project.

SOFT-SIDED MEMORIES: *Fabric Journal Collection Book*

Materials
- inkjet-printable fabric
- fabric, muslin, and fleece
- ultra-sturdy craft interfacing
- permanent inks
- fabric paints
- ball chain
- large grommets
- embellishments (hat pin)
- ribbon
- circle tag
- binding discs
- library pockets
- envelopes (6" x 9" [15.2 x 22.9 cm] and 9" x 12" [22.9 x 30.5 cm])
- card stock
- vintage cloth measuring tape
- waxed linen thread
- brads
- black writing pen

Tools
- sewing machine
- scissors and pinking shears
- craft iron
- awl
- sewing pins
- ½" (1.3 cm) circle punch
- stamps (including alphabet)
- grommet setter
- disc binding punch
- template (page 123)

COLLECTING GENEALOGICAL HISTORY CAN be a time-consuming, albeit enjoyable, process. For the artistically inclined, gathering a family history in one of these collection journals turns the task into an artistic journey. This project uses a disc-binding system so that pages can be added to it quickly and effortlessly. Other methods such as spiral or coil binding could also be used.

Each book can be customized for a specific family and includes a family group sheet (page 123), pockets, envelopes, and places for storing pertinent documentation. For more ways to personalize a collection book, see Making It Personal (page 57).

Let the collective journey start here.

INSTRUCTIONS
Making the Fabric Cover

1. Print photograph onto inkjet-printable fabric and cut out with pinking shears. Cut a piece of fleece slightly smaller than the printed photograph (Fig. 1).

Fig. 1

2. Tear a piece of muslin to approximately 4½" x 7½" (11.4 x 19.1 cm). Wet the muslin and wring it out. Paint and stamp the muslin with the fabric paints and stamps.

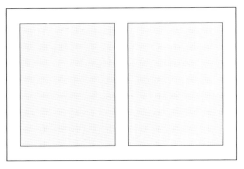

Fig. 2

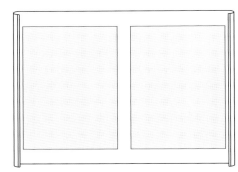

Fig. 3

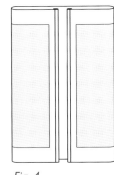

Fig. 4

3. Iron the muslin with a craft iron to dry and flatten. Fray edges if desired. Cut a piece of fleece slightly smaller than the muslin and set aside.

4. Layer the printed photograph over the smaller piece of fleece and sew onto the painted muslin.

5. Cut a piece of fabric 26" (66.0 cm), then sew the muslin to the right half of the right side about 1" to 2" (2.5 to 5.1 cm) from the vertical center (depending on the final size of the muslin) to create the front cover.

6. Cut two pieces of sturdy interfacing to 10" (25.4 cm). With the fabric facedown, lay the short edge of one of the pieces of interfacing ¾" (1.9 cm) from the left edge and centered from top to bottom (Fig. 2).

7. Fold the ¾" (1.9 cm) of fabric over the interfacing and stitch into place (Fig. 3).

8. With the fabric facing up, fold the right edge over 5" (12.7 cm) so that the interfacing is folded in half. Pin in place and repeat with the left side. Sew in place (Fig. 4).

9. Cut off excess material and turn right side out.

10. Use scissors to make a hole in the center of the book cover about ¾" (1.9 cm) from the top edge. Add a grommet.

11. Label the tag and add it to the book with the ball chain. Embellish as desired.

12. Sew a vintage measuring tape (or ribbon) to the spine of the cover.

Making the Book

MAKING A LARGE ENVELOPE DOUBLE POCKET

1. Fold the large envelope in half widthwise and cut ¼" (6 mm) off the folded edge, creating two halves.

2. Follow the binding system instructions to punch the cut edges of the two envelope halves.

3. With the punched side of the bottom half of the envelope on the left side, cut a quarter circle off the top right corner, creating a pocket (Fig. 5).

4. To create the button closure, punch two circles out of the card stock.

5. Use the awl to make a hole through the circle and flap (see Fig. 5 for placement).

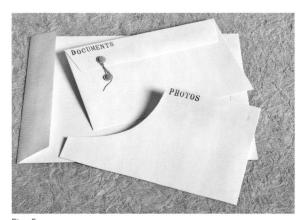

Fig. 5

Finding Inspiration

Originally this journal was just the inside book and I struggled to imagine a cover. I knew I needed something that would protect the binding system and bring an opportunity for personalization. When I realized that paper wasn't going to be both sturdy and flexible enough, I decided to use fabric. Still wanting to add photographs, I immediately thought of the printable fabric sheets I had.

The simple construction of the book cover comes from my days in elementary school when I covered my books with old brown paper bags. When I am in need of inspiration for a new project I sometimes call on long-forgotten materials. The stamped and painted muslin was a happy outcome to a creative experiment with fabric paint I had used for hand lettering on aprons a couple of years before.

6. Put a brad through the hole in the circle and tie a knot around one leg of the brad with an 8" (20.3 cm) piece of waxed linen thread.

7. Place the brad through the hole in the flap.

8. Place a circle on the envelope to the left of the circle on the flap, use the awl to poke a hole, and secure with a brad.

Assembling the Book

1. Punch the two cardboard covers and page elements (library pockets, a copy of the family group sheet, and any envelopes) to be included (Fig. 6).

2. Stamp the outer edge of any page elements if desired.

3. Following the binding system instructions, bind the covers and pages to the discs and slip the book into the fabric cover.

Ancestory

Trudy is the kind of woman who wears her plastic rain bonnet over her head of tightly curled blue hair whenever the chance of precipitation reaches at least 30 percent. She is also the kind of woman who values family. She is, in effect, the family matriarch and historian all rolled into one. Trudy can proudly trace her family tree back seven generations and spends much of her time writing letters to town clerks gathering any bits of information that has somehow managed to elude her.

Trudy's grandson is getting married soon and she is very excited. During a recent visit with Ali, her future granddaughter-in-law, Trudy discovered that Ali was interested in researching her own family ancestry. By the end of the visit the two women had made plans to meet regularly for afternoon tea. This journal is for Ali and Trudy and their new friendship.

Making It Personal: This journal includes pockets for photographs and documentation. What else would you add to customize your book? Other ideas include: land documentation, report cards, educational certifications, maps, grave rubbings, census data, military records, and old correspondence.

Fig. 6

Fanned and Frilly: Altered Board Book

Materials
- board book
- decorative paper
- card stock
- matte medium
- strong double-stick tape
- tacky glue
- glazes and ink
- decorative trim
- ribbon
- photo corners
- photos
- black writing marker
- envelope

Tools
- decorative-edge scallop scissors
- 1/16" (1.6 mm) hole punch
- paper trimmer with scoring blade
- template (page 124)
- brayer or bone folder

Making It Personal: I used decorative paper to create the ruffled trim and card stock for the scalloped lace. For a personal touch, try making your own decorative paper by scanning or copying an old garment. Search in Grandma's sewing box for old lace trim to replace the paper version.

PRETTY *and* PRECOCIOUS IN PINK accurately sums up this handmade historical pop-up book. Fairly simple mechanics and a set of graduated fan charts (page 124) are the stars of this book that humbly started its life as a child's board book. The names on the fan chart were added with a black marker, a steady hand, and a calligraphy book for reference. Using a pencil with a light touch allows even the newest letterer to make a few mistakes before finalizing the names in ink. The ruffled paper and eyelet lace–inspired trim are reminiscent of a little girl's dress and make a fitting theme for a sweet child's heirloom. This book also includes a simple envelope tucked into photo corners on the back page holding a letter of love to the recipient.

INSTRUCTIONS

Preparing the Book

1. Carefully peel the top layer off of the board book pages (Fig. 1).

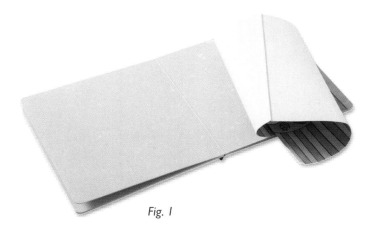

Fig. 1

2. Open the book to the center spread and draw a 1" (2.5 cm) border around the spread. Use a craft knife to cut along this line through all but the first and last page and the front and back cover (Fig. 2).

3. Use the matte medium to adhere the decorative paper to the cover and front-page, center, and back-page spreads. (Use a brayer or a bone folder to help remove any bubbles or wrinkles.)

4. Brush the pages with glaze and rub it in with paper towels. Prop the book open to dry.

Fig.2

Making the Ruffles and Lace

1. Use the paper trimmer with scoring blade to score a sheet of decorative paper at ⅛" (3 mm) and ½" (1.3 cm) alternating intervals.

2. Fold the paper along the score lines in mountain, valley, valley, mountain formation (Fig. 3).

3. Cut the sheet of decorative paper in ¾" (1.9 cm) strips perpendicular to the folds.

4. To create the scallop lace trim, cut ¾" (1.9 cm) strips of card stock with the scallop-edge scissors. Use the 1/16" (1.6 mm) hole punch to punch a hole in each scallop.

Fig. 3

Making the Fan and Cameo

1. Copy the fan template (page 124) onto card stock four times and cut out each level of the fan, leaving the bottom tabs attached.

2. Add the names (and dates if desired) to the fan charts, making sure to leave room for the ruffles.

3. Fold the fans in half, wrong sides together, and fold the bottom tabs to the back.

4. To attach the ruffles to the fan, make a ¼" (6 mm) cut from the bottom of every valley fold (this will allow the bottom to overlap and the top to fan out).

5. Use strong double-stick tape to adhere the ruffles along the back side of each of the fan segments. Add additional strips where necessary.

6. Cut an oval from the card stock and add the lettering to the front. Use the double-stick tape to attach the ruffle and trim to the back of the oval.

Putting It All Together

1. Open the book to the center spread. Glue the scallop trim to the back of the first cut page so that it "borders" the opening about ½" (1.3 cm). Repeat on the back of the last cut page.

2. Glue the ruffle trim between the next two cut pages on the left of the center spread, making sure to not cover up the scallop trim. Repeat on the right side.

3. Glue all the cut pages together on the right side of the center spread. Repeat on the left side.

4. Carefully add adhesive to the largest fan segment tabs and slip the tabs partially between the front page and the glued cut pages on the left, and the last page and the glued pages on the right. The center fold of the fan segment should fall on the center fold of the book, and the center of the fan should sit just a little forward of the two outer points of the fan. Try closing the book once or twice to double-check the placement, making adjustments where necessary.

5. Add the rest of the fan segments one at a time approximately ½" (1.3 cm) in front of each other.

6. Add small photographs with and without photo corners and a quote, if desired, to the center spread.

7. Cut an oval out of the cover slightly larger than the ruffled cameo. Glue the cameo to the front page, making sure it is lined up with the oval cut into the cover.

8. Use the craft knife to cut a small slot in the front and back cover to accommodate the ribbon. Thread the ribbon through these holes.

9. Glaze a piece of decorative paper and let it dry. Trace an opened envelope onto the paper and cut out. Fold into an envelope and tuck a small note or ance*story* inside. Embellish with an extra photograph and attach to the back page with photo corners.

Ance*story*

Our Dearest Lucie,

Oh my! What a beautiful child you are! And how lucky are we to get to meet you. You are still so young with so much to learn and we hope you will be able to learn just a little from us. We know you need to make your own mistakes—both big ones and small ones, but please always remember that we are happy to help whenever you need us.
You come from a very strong family that values education, arts, and personal relationships. We will support you in any endeavor or path you choose. You will never be alone, even if you are far away from us. We will always be in your heart as you will be in ours.
Remember to be kind to others and to always say please and thank you and you'll go a long way in this world.

God Bless,
Great-Grandma Penny, Gran, and Mom

Finding Inspiration

Many times my work is inspired by the challenge of turning an everyday object or "surface" into a piece of art. After packing up a good-sized box of my girls' well-loved but outgrown board books, I realized they might be useful for a future project. Their sturdy pages and rigid binding were the perfect housing for fan chart pop-up. The result is an edgy but pretty little book that opens up revealing a ruffled treasure.

FRAMED AND QUARTERED:
Coin Collector's Book

Materials

- coin collection books
- black and white gesso
- green colored pencils
- white paint pen
- computer-generated list of names
- photographs
- brass embellishments
- hinges
- brads
- heavyweight black art paper
- glazes
- matte medium
- dictionary pages (or copies of clip art, page 126)
- tacky glue
- glue stick
- ink pads
- chalk (optional)
- removable tape

Tools

- awl
- tree template (page 119)

THIS BOOK IS MADE UP of three pages that stand like a room or fireplace screen but they can be easily extended to allow for more family members. The dark flat black and bright flat white surfaces are painted with gessoes, creating a chalklike texture which plays nicely off the vintage photographs. A selection of different hinges and brads hold the pages together with a childlike touch. This family included fifteen children, four of whom passed away as young children or infants. These four are represented with a dove and a heart. While the tree shape may be easily imitated, a template to create this one is provided (page 119).

INSTRUCTIONS

1. Carefully pull apart the collection book elements. Pull the top printed layer off the circle-punched boards. Discard the rest of the book.

2. Paint the front, back, and edges of the circle-punched boards with two coats of black gesso.

3. Use the awl to poke holes and attach the hinges to the boards with brads.

On may 14, 1912, Antwerp, Belgium est children Marie, and S.S. Lapland. They then traveled to settle with Lucie and Augmth $160 and Karel, Louise Bertha Marie. arrived in New York on May 13, 1912 traveled to Capac, their daughter ustus left Antwerp their four young Marie, Zenobie Their ship, the York on May 13, 1912 Michigan to Julia Suzanna.

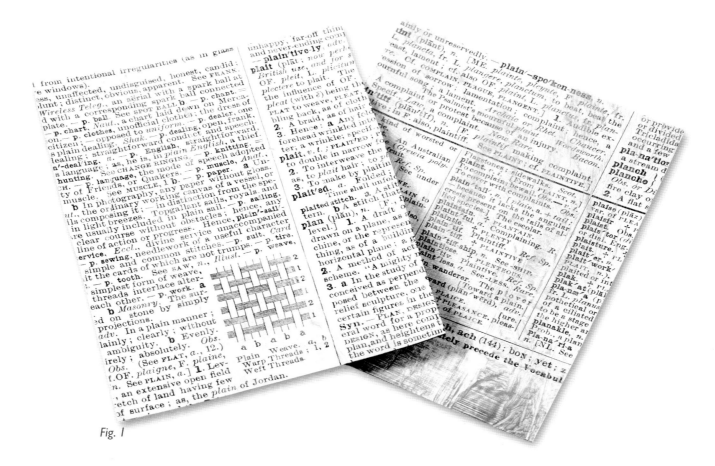

Fig. 1

4. Use matte medium to glue dictionary pages to the art paper. Let this dry and then glaze over the papers with white, cream, and black glazes to make the text less readable (Fig. 1).

5. Cut the glazed art paper to fit the back of each circle board, leaving a ⅛" (3 mm) border around the paper. Use removable tape to temporarily hold the boards in place.

6. Lightly draw a tree shape onto the circle boards with chalk or use a copy of the template (page 119) by rubbing the back of the copy with chalk and then tracing over the copy onto the boards with a pencil to transfer the chalk.

7. Paint the tree shape in with white gesso onto the circle board. Use a second coat if necessary. Mix white glaze with the gesso to create a lighter wash of gesso and fill in the trees in the dictionary openings.

8. Use green pencils to add random leaves, buds, and grass.

9. Age the list of names by running the ink pad over the text, then cut out the names.

10. Cut the photographs into individual silhouettes, and add the photographs and names to the circle openings with the glue stick.

Making It Personal: This family has fifteen children and most families do not. How can you configure your book to fit your family? Try adding spouses or make the tree taller by adding more circle-punched pages to the top. Could you add pages on vertically for additional family trees? Could you honor a generation of great-grandchildren?

11. To create the missing family members, paint gesso onto the brass doves and wipe off, leaving paint in the crevices. Wrap the beginning of the name around the dove branch and cut a decorative tail into the end. Lightly bend the name around a red glazed heart cut from the art paper and glue this into the circle as shown.

12. Remove the tape and glue the circle boards to the art paper backings and weigh down until dry.

13. Place the book facedown and write your ance*story* on the back with a white paint pen.

14. Decorate the bottom of the tree with a red glazed heart and gessoed brass findings. Date if desired.

Ance*story*

On May 4, 1912, Lucie and Augustus left Antwerp, Belgium, with $160 and their four youngest children, Karl, Louise Marie, Zenobie Marie, and Bertha Marie. Their ship, the S.S. Lapland, arrived in New York on May 13, 1912. They then traveled on to Capac, Michigan, to settle with their daughter Julia Suzanna Gheldof.

Finding Inspiration

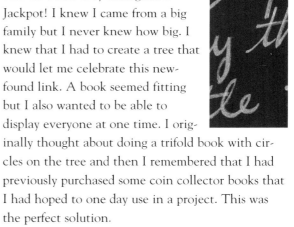

This project was inspired by a photograph that was happened upon by chance on the Internet. While doing a search for my mother's maiden name a site appeared that seemed to be listing a link to my great-great-grandmother, for whom my mother was named. I immediately followed the link to see if what I hoped was true. There on my laptop screen appeared a photograph of my great-great-grandparents and eleven of their fifteen children. There were also names and dates and information on when they immigrated. Jackpot! I knew I came from a big family but I never knew how big. I knew that I had to create a tree that would let me celebrate this new-found link. A book seemed fitting but I also wanted to be able to display everyone at one time. I originally thought about doing a trifold book with circles on the tree and then I remembered that I had previously purchased some coin collector books that I had hoped to one day use in a project. This was the perfect solution.

Hiding Jacob's Ladder:
Wooden Book and Shrine

Materials
- wooden box and wooden plaque
- ribbon
- old music book pages (see clip art, page 125)
- copper wire (20- and 24-gauge)
- balsa wood
- carpet tacks and small nails
- card stock
- matte medium
- acrylic glaze
- acrylic polymer (GAC 100)
- paper towels
- optometrist lens
- small and extra-small wood knobs
- four wooden spindles or legs
- glue
- 2" (5.1 cm) photographs printed on inkjet transparencies in reverse
- spray-on fixative
- absorbent ground
- copper tape
- decorative paper and small collage ephemera
- ink

Tools
- drill with bits
- detail paintbrush
- alphabet stamps
- craft knife

THIS PLAYFUL BOOK COMES with its own case and four legs to stand on. Small panels of wood are covered with vintage children's book pages and interlaced with hand-dyed silk ribbon to create a moveable book. Small transparent photo collages are tucked into alternating pages that can flip up with the aid of a decorative wooden knob mounted on the cover. A coordinating wooden box with its lid removed is decked out in copper wire, glazes, and an optometrist's lens, making a perfect hiding place for this whimsical Jacob's ladder project.

INSTRUCTIONS
Making the Shrine
1. Remove the top of the wooden box and reserve for another project. Coat the box and the wooden plaque with the acrylic polymer and let it dry.

2. Cover the outside of the box, the wooden plaque, legs, and knobs with a coat of glaze. Use a paper towel to rub the glaze into the wood and to remove the excess glaze.

3. Use matte medium to decoupage old (music) book pages to the inside of the box.

4. Insert carpet tacks into the holes from the box hardware. Wrap the box bottom with the 20-gauge copper wire as shown in the photograph. (Use the nails to loop the wire.)

5. Glue the wooden plaque to the top of the box.

6. Use a craft knife to cut out a heart from the balsa wood. Carefully carve the heart and glaze it. Do not rub off the excess glaze.

7. Use old book text or computer-generated text to create a phrase for the lens. Attach the phrase to the back of the lens with matte medium.

8. Wrap wire around the heart and attach it to the lens. Use wire and a nail to hang the lens from the top of the shrine.

Preparing the Book

1. Cut twelve pieces of wood to 2½" x 3" (6.4 x 7.6 cm). Cover one side of each of the pieces with old (music) book pages.

2. On one of the panels drill four holes to accommodate the legs.

3. Glue the smaller knob to the top of the bigger knob.

4. Cut the ribbon into three pieces about 25" (63.5 cm) in length.

Constructing the Book

1. Divide the wood panels into six pairs (each pair has one top and one bottom panel).

2. Lay the top and bottom ribbon horizontally and set the bottom panel of the first pair good side down about 1" (2.5 cm) from the left side of the ribbon. Overlap the middle ribbon 1" (2.5 cm) onto the middle of the right side of the panel. Glue the top panel down to the bottom panel (Fig.1).

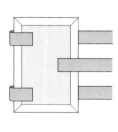

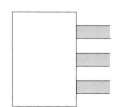

Fig. I

3. Slip the bottom of the next pair of panels over the middle ribbon and under the top and bottom ribbon. Fold the middle ribbon to the left. Glue the top panel for this pair over the bottom panel (Fig. 2).

4. Fold the top and bottom ribbon to the left and the middle ribbon to the right over the last glued pair of panels. Place the bottom of the next pair facedown over the ribbons. Fold the top and bottom ribbons to the right and the middle ribbon to the left. Glue the top panel for this pair over the bottom panel (Fig. 3).

5. Flip the last panel over to the right and repeat steps 3 and 4.

6. Flip the last panel over and slip the bottom of the last panel (without the feet) over the top and bottom ribbon and under the middle ribbon. Trim the ribbons and fold the top and bottom ribbons to the left. Glue the last top panel over the ribbons (Fig. 4).

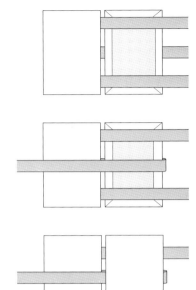

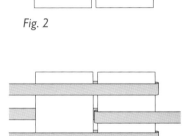

Fig. 2

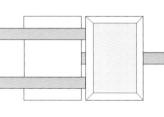

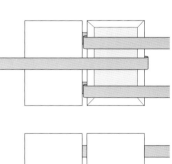

Fig. 3

7. Carefully fold the book and place a weight on top of it until the glue dries.

Making the Photo Collages

1. Lightly spray the printed side of the transparencies with fixative.

2. Use a small brush to paint one or two coats of absorbent ground to the subject of the photograph on the printed side (Fig. 5).

Fig. 4

Fig. 5

3. Cut 2" (5.1 cm) of card stock and collage with bits of ephemera, decorative paper, and book text (Fig. 6).

Fig.6

Ance*story*

Bob and Lucy seem to be perpetual parents; no matter how many years pass, there always seem to be little ones toddling around the family room. After raising four children they extended their family by adopting two more fabulous children and fostering another forty-eight.

Their immediate family now is up to sixteen including four very energetic grandchildren under the age of seven. All four grandchildren are now living some distance from their Papa Bob and Granma Lu but they do their best to send email and pictures, cards, and bright crayon drawings. Never were there two more loving grandparents. If you ever stop by their home, make sure you ask to see the pictures.

4. Attach the picture to the card stock with copper tape.

5. Stamp the ribbon with names if desired and then attach the photographs to the page with glue. Weigh the book down until dry and then glue the knob to the top of the book.

LIBRARY OF RELATIVES:
Mini Journals Collection

Materials
- hardcover book
- decorative paper
- watercolor or text-woven artist paper
- card stock
- eyelets
- ribbons
- watercolor pencils
- small watercolor brush
- black writing pen
- photographs and ephemera
- quotes (page 75)

Tools
- eyelet setter
- metal ruler (I like to use an 18" [45.7 cm] or 36" [91.4 cm])
- anywhere hole punch
- craft knife
- bone folder

MOST OF THE PROJECTS in this book are designed to showcase a little information about a lot of relatives, but these mini journals serve as a vehicle for creatively logging other "related" information, photographs, and sketches. Uniquely encased inside an old hardcover with eyelets and ribbons, each mini journal can be slipped out and added to as new information is discovered or verified. Add old dance cards, report cards, land documents, or just photographs. To make this a quick project I used my favorite black writing marker, watercolor pencils, and quotes to decorate the pages of my mini journals.

INSTRUCTIONS
Making the Hardcover

1. Use a craft knife to cut the pages out of the book where the endpapers meet the spine. (Be careful not to cut through the cover.)

2. Measure the inside of the spine and cut a piece of decorative paper about ¼" (6 mm) shorter and 2" (5.1 cm) wider and glue this into the spine for reinforcement.

3. Add a row of eyelets ¼" (6 mm) from the top and the bottom of the spine, making sure to space them evenly.

4. To determine the length of your ribbon, measure the distance from the top and bottom row of eyelets, multiply this by the number of eyelets, and add 12" (30.5 cm).

Fig. 1

5. Starting on the outside of the spine, lace the ribbon through the eyelets, making sure the ribbon goes from top to bottom on the inside of the spine and diagonally on the outside. Bring the ends to the middle of the spine on the outside and tie around all the ribbons to create an hourglass shape as shown in the photograph.

Making the Mini Journals

1. To determine the size of the mini journal, measure the front cover of the book. The finished journal should be approximately ½" (1.3 cm) shorter and ¼" (6 mm) narrower than this measurement.

2. Cut a piece of card stock to the height of the finished journal and two times the width plus 3" to 4" (7.6 to 10.2 cm) (this may depend on the width of the card stock being used).

3. Use a bone folder to fold the card stock in half widthwise. To make the fold on the front cover, measure and mark the finished journal width from the middle fold and make a fold at this mark. Repeat for the back of the cover (Fig. 1).

Finding Inspiration

Old books can be delightfully revitalized to house family history projects. Be sure to avoid moldy ones; smell them at flea markets and antique shops like you would smell a cantaloupe at a farmers market. I seek out vintage books on homekeeping and etiquette because I get a kick out of reading through them. Other features to consider are unique pictures, size, and color.

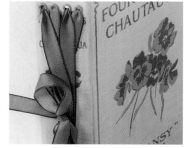

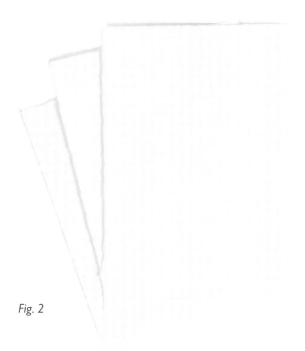

Fig. 2

Variation IDEAS

- *Create a whole encyclopedia set of mini journals or use a large tome to hold a large family.*

- *Vary the ribbon used to tie each mini journal.*

- *Add more pages to extend a mini journal.*

- *Use a mini journal on its own to give as a gift.*

- *Send mini journals to family members to fill out and return for a personal keepsake.*

Fig. 3

Fig. 4

4. The journal pages will be ½" (1.3 cm) shorter than the finished journal height and two times wider minus ½" (1.3 cm). Use the metal ruler to tear strips of the watercolor paper to size, creating deckled-edged pages. Three pages are needed for each mini journal (Fig. 2).

5. To make a hole guide, cut a 2" (5.1 cm) strip of scrap card stock to the height of the finished mini journal. Fold it in half lengthwise and punch three holes in it—one in the center and one ¾" (1.9 cm) from the top and from the bottom along the fold (Fig. 3).

6. Center three journal pages onto a journal cover and clip the hole guide securely to the center of the journal (Fig. 4).

7. Punch through the top and bottom holes and remove the pages. Use the guide to punch the center hole only through the cover. Punch two more holes halfway down the front and back folds. (This is where the ribbon comes through to tie the journal closed.)

Fig. 5

8. Cut a piece of ribbon six times the height of the mini journal. Insert the pages back into the journal and lace the ribbon evenly through both holes.

9. Flip the journal over and insert both ends of the ribbon back through the center hole while guiding one toward the front cover and one toward the back cover. Pull these ends through the holes along the front and back folded edge (Fig. 5).

10. Use photographs, ephemera, watercolor pencils, black writing markers, and quotes to decorate the mini journals (Fig. 6).

11. Open the journals to the center spread and slide under a ribbon in the hardcover to complete the collection.

Making It Personal: The books I used for this project were chosen first for their color, size, and condition and second for their interesting covers. What type of book would you choose for your family? Foreign titles? Shakespeare's plays? Old cookbooks? Think about how the titles you chose can reflect the people documented inside the journals.

Fig. 6

Ance*story*

Telling your story with quotations …

A child is a curly, dimpled lunatic.
—RALPH WALDO EMERSON

Mothers are fonder than fathers of their children because they are more certain they are their own.
—ARISTOTLE

The reason grandparents and grandchildren get along so well is that they have a common enemy.
—SAM LEVENSON

It is not flesh and blood but the heart which makes us fathers and sons.
—JOHANN SCHILLER

We all grow up with the weight of history on us. Our ancestors dwell in the attics of our brains as they do in the spiraling chains of knowledge hidden in every cell of our bodies.
—SHIRLEY ABBOTT

The happiest moments of my life have been the few which I have passed at home in the bosom of my family.
—THOMAS JEFFERSON

The informality of family life is a blessed condition that allows us to become our best while looking our worst.
—MARGE KENNEDY

Other things may change us, but we start and end with the family.
—ANTHONY BRANDT

Family faces are magic mirrors. Looking at people who belong to us, we see the past, present and future.
—GAIL LUMET BUCKLEY

I don't have to look up my family tree because I know that I'm the sap.
—FRED ALLEN

Sometimes being a brother is even better than being a superhero.
—MARC BROWN

It takes two men to make one brother.
—ISRAEL ZANGWILL

Some mothers are kissing mothers and some are scolding mothers, but it is love just the same, and most mothers kiss and scold together.
—PEARL S. BUCK

The heart of a mother is a deep abyss at the bottom of which you will always find forgiveness.
—HONORÉ DE BALZAC

Women are aristocrats, and it is always the mother who makes us feel that we belong to the better sort.
—JOHN LANCASTER SPALDING

A truly rich man is one whose children run into his arms when his hands are empty.
—AUTHOR UNKNOWN

Sometimes the poorest man leaves his children the richest inheritance.
—RUTH E. RENKEL

What's the good of news if you haven't a sister to share it?
—JENNY DEVRIES

Sisters function as safety nets in a chaotic world simply by being there for each other.
—CAROL SALINE

Our brothers and sisters are there with us from the dawn of our personal stories to the inevitable dusk.
—SUSAN SCARF MERRELL

What a bargain grandchildren are! I give them my loose change, and they give me a million dollars' worth of pleasure.
—GENE PERRET

Perfect love sometimes does not come until the first grandchild.
—WELSH PROVERB

Our grandchildren accept us for ourselves, without rebuke or effort to change us, as no one in our entire lives has ever done, not our parents, siblings, spouses, friends—and hardly ever our own grown children.
—RUTH GOODE

Grandchildren don't stay young forever, which is good because Poppops have only so many horsey rides in them.
—GENE PERRET

When grandparents enter the door, discipline flies out the window.
—OGDEN NASH

Grandma always made you feel she had been waiting to see just you all day and now the day was complete.
—MARCY DeMAREE

Chapter Four
TREE HOUSES: Three-Dimensional Family Trees

Sadie's Girls, page 78

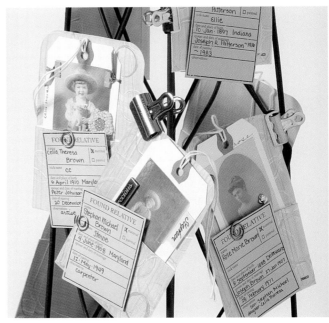

It's All Relatives, page 82

Possibly the most challenging way of designing a family tree, creating in three dimensions, offers the ability to showcase a piece on a table or bookshelf out in the open—a true conversation piece. The projects in this chapter are inspired by things such as English gardens, *The Nutcracker Suite*, and walks by the sea, and feature interesting materials including plaster cloth, hardware cloth, sea fans, and topiary forms.

Sadie's Girls: Paper and Wire Sculpture is one of those easy and delightfully messy projects that harkens back to days in elementary school and papier-mâché science fair projects. This time we're using pieces of plaster cloth that stiffen into something hard and durable. It's like making magic in the studio.

It's All Relatives: Paper Topiary Tree handsomely holds random bits of information and snapshots of time in gelatin-printed library pockets. No need to know your entire family tree to get started here; just a few pictures, a pot, and a trellis will do.

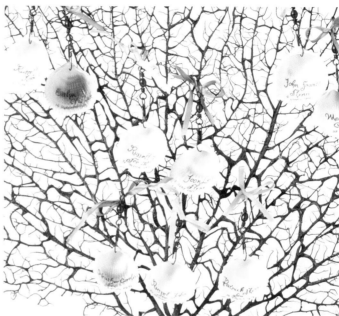

Mossy Mementos, page 86

My Family by the Sea, page 90

Mossy Mementos: Standing History Wreath
happens to be another great project to commemorate one special generation. This time, instead of highlighting the grandchildren, the focus is turned back two generations to the grandparents. Who doesn't love a baby face?

You can almost hear the ocean with **My Family by the Sea: Sea Fan Assemblage.** A simple construction frame houses an intriguing piece of sea life. Decorated with shells and illustrations on the inside and poetry on the outside, this project is an ocean breeze.

So think outside the box and delve into the third dimension. If you get stuck, take a break to visit the art museum or the local home décor store. Look for inspiration in color, texture, and materials to guide your next family tree. With any luck, you'll be inspired to create something with your own unique supplies to add to the list of three-dimensional possibilities.

SADIE'S GIRLS:
Paper and Wire Sculpture

Materials
- papier-mâché torso
- hardware cloth (¼" square openings) cut 17½" x 17½" (44.5 x 44.5 cm)
- 16-gauge wire
- plaster cloth
- decorative paper
- old sheet music
- fluid acrylics, acrylic paints, and glazes in desired colors
- matte gel medium
- gesso
- ribbon
- hat pin
- wooden disks approximately 1" (2.5 cm) wide
- 12 mm jump rings
- black writing marker
- paper towels

Tools
- round-nosed pliers
- wire cutters
- tin snips
- paintbrushes (foam and small detail size)
- drill and small bit (5⁄64" [2 mm] will work)
- large bowl with water
- work gloves (optional for cutting hardware cloth)

AT FIRST THIS PROJECT looks difficult because of its three-dimensionality, but in truth it harkens back to the easy days of kindergarten creating piñatas and papier-mâché art. The premade papier-mâché torso is quickly wrapped in a large rectangle of hardware cloth, setting the stage for the truly fun part—the plaster cloth. If you have little ones in your life and have the option of including them in this project, this is the perfect time to do so! Your young protégés will enjoy watching the plaster cloth turn from dry, flexible cloth to soggy, drippy cloth to a hard castlike dress shell.

This piece pays homage to a great family matriarch and her direct female descendants (see Finding Inspiration, page 81). The mobile was constructed and added to show the line of descendants and to give the piece movement.

INSTRUCTIONS
Recipe for Construction
Creating the base and configuring the mobile are the most complicated parts of this fun piece. Take your time cutting out the hardware cloth, cutting as close to the wire intersections as possible to prevent sharp edges.

Making the Sculpture
1. Paint the torso and the wooden disks with a coat of gesso and let dry.

2. Wrap the hardware cloth around the waist of the torso and secure with short lengths of wire where the hardware cloth overlaps and a longer piece of wire running from the front of the skirt to the back to hold the torso in place (Fig. 1).

3. Slightly bend the two outside corners of the skirt up.

4. Cut the plaster cloth into small workable strips. Following manufacturer's instructions, dip the strips into the bowl of water and cover the hardware cloth on the outside and the inside (Fig. 2). Make sure to wrap the edges of the wire as well, making a seamless transition from the torso to the skirt.
Note: It will be necessary for the outside to dry before covering the inside to keep the plaster cloth from falling off.

5. After the skirt has dried, tear the decorative paper into strips of varying sizes and use slightly watered-down gel medium and the foam brush to adhere the pieces to the skirt. Set aside some smaller pieces for the torso.

6. Tear pieces of sheet music and cover the torso and the inside of the skirt in the same manner as step 5. Mix small pieces of decorative paper and sheet music to make a transition around the waist of the sculpture.

7. Use a mixture of glazes, fluid acrylics, and acrylic paints to lightly color the sculpture on the inside and outside. Brush the paints on and then wipe off the excess color with a paper towel.

8. Cut a length of ribbon for a sash if desired and add letters with a detail brush and acrylic paint. Attach the ribbon to the form with a hat pin.

Making the Mobile

1. Plan out the mobile on a piece of paper. Each gessoed wooden disk will need a hole drilled at the top and the bottom to accept a jump ring, except for the last descendent on each line, which will only need a hole at the top.

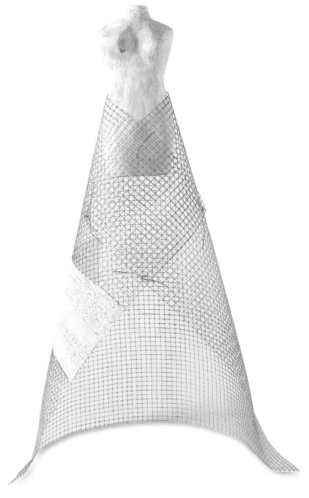

Fig. I

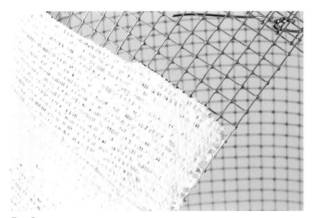

Fig. 2

Ancestory

Sadie was a woman filled with quick Irish wit and ingenuity. She arrived in the States around 1916 and raised a house full of wonderful children. Because of an illness in her twenties, Sadie became prematurely white haired and seems to be remembered as the consummate grandmother. She always wore Tabu perfume and an apron. Due to poor-fitting dentures that she chose not to wear (but kept in her apron at the ready in case of an unexpected visitor), she had a wrinkly soft face. She was known to amaze the grandchildren with her smoke rings from cigarettes that she always claimed to never inhale. Some remember her telling the story of stone soup whenever it was requested, and some remember her sitting on the back lawn twirling her thumbs. Regardless, she loved her family and was well loved in return.

Finding Inspiration

This piece was initially inspired by my love of dress forms, which stems from my early introduction to sewing. Once the dress form/torso entered my subconscious I soon started seeing images of *The Nutcracker Suite* and the Mother Ginger character where all the dancers come out from under her skirt. Color was again an inspiration for me as I chose to represent the colors present on the flag of Ireland where Sadie came from before crossing the Atlantic Ocean to live in America. The sheet music was used to represent the songs that Sadie was known to hum.

2. Using the black marker, add any information desired to the disks. (This information could also be printed on the computer and cut to fit the disks.) I chose to use the first and middle name on the front and the birth date and profession on the back.

3. Use a foam brush and a number of glazes and/or fluid acrylics to tint the wooden disks.

4. To keep the mobile balanced, start at the bottom and work up. If there is only one disk hanging, connect it to the disk above with a jump ring. If there are two or more disks hanging, a crossbar will need to be created. Lay the disks next to each other and measure the distance from the middle of the first one to the middle of the last one. Cut the wire a little longer than this to start.

5. With the round-nosed pliers, make a loop on the left end of the wire and then add another loop along the wire at each point that another disk should hang (Fig. 3).

Fig. 3

6. There will also need to be a loop to attach the crossbar to the disk above. Depending on the number of disks, this loop for above may difficult to place. Try resting the crossbar with all its hanging disks attached on your finger until you find the balancing point. This is where to add your hanging loop.

7. Continue working up to the top of the mobile, ending with a jump ring in the top wooden disk or in a balanced center wire loop (depending on your specific layout).

8. Cut a piece of wire long enough to hang the mobile inside the skirt. Make a loop on one end and attach this to the top jump ring. Bend the top of the wire over to create a hook, and hook it to the inside front of the skirt, making sure the mobile can move freely.

IT'S ALL RELATIVES:
Paper Topiary Tree

Materials
- old book pages
- metal trellis form
- planter
- reindeer moss
- green floral foam (enough to fill the planter)
- floral pins
- gloss medium
- acrylic glazes
- fluid acrylics
- small binder clips
- library pockets (See Making It Your Own, page 85)
- office tags
- card stock
- label template (page 125)
- miscellaneous embellishments
- fasteners such as paper clips and staples
- photographs
- string or ribbon

Tools
- craft knife
- small paintbrush

THIS TREE IS DEFINITELY the one to try first if you keep getting random photographs from great-aunt Sally and your mother-in-law. Just one pocket at a time helps to create a tree full of relatives without having to organize them and fill in the blanks. Little "Found Relative" tags can be clipped on to help label the photographs. The pockets, decorated with an interesting gelatin printing technique (see Making It Your Own, page 85), can hold all sorts of doodads and whatnots. An inexpensive tin planter is decoupaged with interesting book pages and accented with glazes to finish off the fanciful look.

INSTRUCTIONS

1. Decorate the tags with photographs and embellishments.

2. Copy the label onto card stock and attach a label and decorated tag to each library pocket. (To use painted pockets, see Making It Your Own.)

3. Use old book pages to decorate the planter by adhering the pages with gloss medium.

4. Lightly brush the covered planter with touches of glaze.

5. Dip the bottoms of the paint and glaze bottles into the paint, and glaze and stamp circles onto the planter.

6. Insert the floral foam into the planter, using a craft knife to trim the foam where necessary.

7. Use floral pins to secure the moss to the foam, and carefully insert the trellis into the planter.

8. Use the binder clips to attach the pockets to the trellis.

9. Cut a tag into a flag shape, and add a family name if desired. Tie the tag to the top of the trellis.

Finding Inspiration

The trellis in this project was originally used to hold Christmas tree lights in the winter but in an attempt to downsize in a recent move I decided to donate it. Fate, however, stepped in (my husband misunderstood which pile it was assigned) and it was mistakenly put in my studio. I labeled it with a note "to be donated" so this wouldn't happen again. A few days later I was looking at the trellis form with its note clipped on and thought to myself that it might make a great memo board—a holder for handmade art and cards. So I grabbed a library pocket that was just thrown on my studio table and clipped it on as well … and the wheels started to spin.

Ancestory

Angela likes to shop for a family. She is an only child and always wanted a brother or sister. So now she likes to go looking for them in old bins and baskets at flea markets and antique stores. She likes to pick out ones that tell a story. An old man with a great mustache, a little baby boy whose eyes must have been light blue, a woman in glasses that had to have been a Mildred or an Estelle—all become Angela's family. How sad, she thinks, that these people have all been forgotten or lost to their family. Now they will be loved and wondered about, and given names, stories, husbands, wives, children. They are not forgotten.

Making It Your Own

Creating Gelatin-Printed Library Pockets

Gelatin printing is used here to decorate library pockets but could easily be used to decorate beautiful background papers, tags, cards, and so on. Try using different tools to make impressions in the paint before printing. Lay small items such as feathers or rubber bands onto the paint-coated gelatin before printing for an interesting effect. Take time to experiment; the results can be fascinating.

Suggested Materials

- 8" (20.3 cm) square disposable aluminum tin, three gelatin packages, water, brayer, fluid acrylics and glazes, small Plexiglas (for rolling out the paints, card stock, scissors

1. Follow the instructions on the gelatin packages for making gelatin blocks, substituting water for fruit juice. Use all three packages and pour the mixed gelatin into the aluminum tin. Let the gelatin set up in the refrigerator until firm.

2. Lay a thin line of fluid acrylic onto the Plexiglas, and use the brayer to roll out the paint until the brayer is evenly covered.

3. Evenly roll the brayer over the gelatin until it is covered with the fluid acrylic.

4. Lightly press the circular bottoms of the glazes and fluid acrylics into the acrylic-covered gelatin to create a pattern.

5. Carefully lay a library pocket facedown into the paint and gently apply pressure over the back of the pocket. Repeat with all the pockets and the back sides if desired.

Fig. I

6. Create a texture tool by making ¼" (6 mm) -deep cuts every ⅛" (3 mm) along one side of a small piece of card stock (Fig. 1).

7. Repeat steps 2 and 3 using a complementary glaze color. Lightly run the texture tool over the paint to create a striped surface on the gelatin. Carefully lay a library pocket facedown into the paint and gently apply pressure over the back of the pocket. Repeat with all the pockets and the back sides if desired.

8. Dip the bottoms of the paint bottles into a fluid acrylic and then stamp them on to the library pockets.

Making It Personal: Although this trellis is strewn with pockets of people, it could easily be changed up for the season. Do you have a collection of photograph Christmas cards received from family? How about celebrating spring with family members' names written on paper flowers and tied to the trellis? How would you prune this topiary?

Mossy Mementos:
Standing History Wreath

Materials
- rolled sheet moss
- floral pins
- 12" (30.5 cm) floral foam wreath
- balsa wood 3½" (8.9 cm) and ½" (1.3 cm) wide
- canvas
- absorbent ground for pastels
- brass knobs
- brass nameplates
- mini brass screws
- carpet and upholstery tacks
- ribbon ¼" (6 mm) wide
- velvet ribbon ½" (1.3 cm) wide
- vine ribbon trim
- paper flowers
- brown chisel-tip marker
- blending marker or wintergreen oil and cotton ball
- picture stand
- tacky glue
- copier or laser prints of the photographs
- colored pencils

Tools
- staple gun with staples
- mini screwdriver
- palette knife
- craft knife
- metal ruler
- bone folder

THIS FAMILY TREE STANDS on its own, literally. Using a picture stand to hold the wreath allows the family of honor to be celebrated out in the open, not just on a door or over a fireplace (although this could easily hang as well.) Image transfers of baby pictures that represent a single generation gone by could easily become a two-generation family of five or six. Tiny canvases hang from diminutive brass knobs on this wreath of moss and velvet ribbon. Rolled moss sheets, available at craft stores, are unrolled and quickly tacked to a foam wreath form with floral pins, creating a blank surface. Thin, easy-to-cut balsa wood becomes a nameplate ledge for the stretched, prepared, and hand-colored portraits. Finishing touches such as vine-shaped ribbon, paper flowers, and upholstery tacks make this wreath even sweeter.

INSTRUCTIONS

1. Unroll the sheet moss and roll it around the wreath form, securing it with floral pins. Make sure to cover the entire wreath.

2. Use the velvet ribbon and floral pins to create a crisscross pattern on the wreath as shown in the photograph.

3. Use a craft knife and metal ruler to score and cut the larger balsa wood into five 3" x 2½" (7.6 x 6.4 cm) pieces.

The Hahn Children

Ellie
1910–2001

George
1913–1986

Clyde
1915–2004

Joseph
1911–1969

Grace
1908–1997

4. Cut or tear the canvas into five pieces approximately 5" by 4½" (12.7 cm x 11.4 cm). Lay one of the pieces of balsa on top of one of the pieces of canvas, wrap the corner in tightly, and secure with the staple gun (Fig. 1).

5. Carefully pull in each side, making sure to tuck the corner in neatly to reduce the bulk, and secure with the staple gun.

6. Repeat with the remaining wood and canvas.

Fig. 1

7. Use the palette knife to add a thin layer of absorbent ground to each of the stretched canvases.

8. When the ground has dried, place one of the copied photographs facedown on top of one of the canvases. Use either the blending marker or the wintergreen oil on a cotton ball and gently cover the back of the photograph, making sure to keep the photograph from moving. When the photograph has been saturated, use a bone folder to burnish the back of the photograph and then slowly pull up one corner to see if the image has transferred as desired. If not, apply more marker or oil and burnish again.

9. Use the colored pencils to lightly hand color the photographs.

10. Cut five 3" (7.6 cm) pieces of balsa for the ledges and stain them with the brown marker. Use the tacky glue to attach them to the canvas bottoms.

11. Trim the top and sides with strips of velvet ribbon and then attach a hanging ribbon with two upholstery tacks.

12. Use glue to attach snippets of vine to the canvas before screwing in the nameplates with names inserted.

13. Add paper flowers if desired.

14. Attach the canvases to the wreath with mini brass knobs.

Making It Personal: This wreath is sweet and lovely with baby photographs of an earlier generation. What other pieces of your family could you hang among the moss? Could you commemorate those family members who've served in the military? Use red velvet ribbon and armed services embellishments. Add their military rank to the nameplate and show them how much you appreciate their sense of duty.

15. To create the nameplate, cut a piece of the left-over balsa to approximately 1" (2.5 cm) longer and wider than your brass nameplate and stain it with the brown marker.

16. Tear a piece of canvas just a little smaller than the balsa and fray the edges. Glue this to the wood and add vine and floral details.

17. Attach the brass nameplate and name to the wooden plaque with ribbon and carpet tacks. Wrap the extra ribbon to the back and secure to the wreath with glue.

18. Tie a bow with the velvet ribbon and attach with a floral pin under the wreath.

19. Prop up the wreath in the display stand.

Ance*story*

Kirsten was helping her grandfather organize and sort through old paperwork on a crisp fall day. Dressed in layers of wool sweaters, the two of them rummaged through old trunks and boxes to discover newspapers, greeting cards, love letters, and photographs that her grand-mother had saved. In a small metal box with a broken lock, Kirsten found photographs tied with an old ribbon. On the top of the stack was a note in her grandmother's handwriting that said, "The Hahn Children." Even though her grandfather could pick out her grandmoth-er's picture from the stack, Kirsten checked the back of each photograph to read the lacy hand-writing that labeled each child: George, Ellie, Clyde, Joseph, and Grace, her grandmother. Her grandfather placed his hands on top of the photographs she was gingerly holding and told her, "They are yours now, she would want you to have them."

Finding Inspiration

This little wreath was inspired by a process. I wanted to use small canvases in a project in a unique way and was immediately drawn to transfer-ring images to them. I knew I'd run in to difficulties trying to transfer images to standard mini canvases because of their construction. I decided to try to invent a way to stretch a mini canvas so that it would be easy to construct and solid to transfer onto. The result of trial and error was to use small pieces of balsa, easily cut with a craft knife and ruler. Once the mini canvases were invented, they needed a place to hang. Originally I thought of a mobile but felt the construction would be too diffi-cult to translate. Later, while thumbing through a home furnishings catalog, I saw a stand for a wreath. This was the perfect solution for the mini canvases and the final piece to my puzzle—a standing wreath.

My Family by the Sea:
Sea Fan Assemblage

Materials
- sea fan
- basswood ¼" x 4" (6 mm x 10.2 cm) for the base
- basswood ¼" x 3" (6 mm x 7.6 cm) for the frame
- basswood trim ¼" x ⅜" (6 mm x 1 cm)
- decorative paper with seashells
- seashells
- interlock snap swivels (available from fishing tackle store)
- hand-dyed silk ribbon
- black writing marker
- eight 2" (5.1 cm) brass flat corner braces
- glazes
- matte medium
- white acrylic paint
- white paint pen
- acrylic polymer (GAC 100)
- Gorilla Glue
- tacky craft glue

Tools
- small wood craft saw (or scroll/band saw)
- hand drill and small bit
- pliers
- screwdriver
- craft knife
- small paintbrush

SEA FANS ARE A TYPE of coral that grows in the ocean perpendicular to the current to catch its dinner. But to this project a sea fan is a family tree—a collector of relatives. Small hand-lettered shells are hung from fishing snap swivels and small streamers of hand-dyed silk ribbons. Encased in a sturdy, yet airy frame, the "tree" stands proudly surrounded by the ancestory of this family written as poetry. Illustrations of sea life grace the inside shadows of the frame under a milky haze of white glaze. The frame is easily constructed with basswood from a craft store, a small craft saw, and hand drill. Brass flat corner braces hold everything together with a little help of some super-strong glue. This sea fan will surely garner fans of its own.

INSTRUCTIONS

1. Measure your sea fan and cut two of the 3" (7.6 cm) boards just slightly wider than the width of the fan (these are the top and bottom of the frame). Cut two more of the boards 2" (5.1 cm) taller than the fan (these are the two side frames). Cut the 4" (10.2 cm) -wide base board 1" (2.5 cm) longer than the top and bottom boards.

2. Coat each of the boards on all sides with acrylic polymer and then with a thin coat of acrylic paint. (The polymer acts as a primer and protects the paint from being discolored by the wood.)

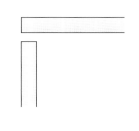

Fig. 1

3. Overlap the ends of the frame pieces to assemble (Fig. 1). Use the flat corner braces to attach the pieces at the corners. Use the hand drill to start a pilot hole for the screws to keep the wood from splitting. Attach a brace on both sides of all four corners.

4. Cut out the illustrated seashells and use the matte medium to decoupage them to the inside of the frame. Trim the illustrations where necessary.

5. Use a loose mixture of white and off-white glazes to paint over the illustrations. Let the first coat dry before adding the second coat.

6. With a blue glaze and a small paintbrush, add the poem to the outside of the frame, keeping the letters loose and big (Fig. 2).

7. When the glaze has fully dried, use the white paint pen to write the poem a second time. This time use smaller, tighter handwriting (Fig. 3).

8. When the paint pen has fully dried, use the black writing marker to write the full poem on the outside of the frame.

9. Use the hand drill to carefully drill a hole in the tops of the seashells for hanging. Add an interlock snap swivel, using the pliers if necessary.

Fig. 2

Fig. 3

10. Write the family names in the shells with the black writing marker. (Use a typeface from a computer or a calligraphy book as a guide.)

11. Use a craft knife to carve out a small hole in the base of the sea fan. Cut a piece of the basswood trim to about 2½" to 3" (6.4 cm to 7.6 cm), paint it white, and insert it into the hole in the fan with Gorilla Glue. Let dry completely.

Ance*story*

My Family by the Sea:
Naval Cadet Meets His Bride-to-Be at the Beach

"Whites and wings, they have all the glamour,"
—said of Navy pilots in the 1940s

Mary came up in her skirted two-piece
asking for a picture with a girlfriend, new
camera from her father who couldn't come, heart
attack laid him up in bed. Trip planned for weeks, beach
house already hired. Her mom said, "Go ahead;
take a friend," and they set out driving.

Changed course mid-way, headed for Hampton
instead of White Horse. Hired house lay
empty and John lay waiting, propped up on one elbow
in his Navy-issue woolen briefs, ankles crossed in the sand
taking a little R&R, salt pre-maturely dusting
his hair white above raven brows.

"Sure," he said and snapped her picture, lustrous
movie-star locks, top half of her suit tied up
somewhere under those brunette waves, dark lips,
slim arms wrapped around her knees,
her friend, giggly, giddy from the sight of trim
cadets, John and his friend, just
old enough to vote, but already adults.

That night he and she took a walk, water glowed with
phosphorus, the ancient name for Venus, love and the full
moon, old story made new by the urgency of war.
* One thousand*
stars emerged, not reflections, but new lights in their own
right, released by oxygen and turbulence, the wake of a
* ship or limbs*
pulling through ocean tide. She took him home to
her family; "We saw each other every night that week;
* and one*
year after we met, seven to ten dates later, we were
* married."*

How normal it seemed then to leap
begin a new life before the old one had faded, he not
yet a pilot, whites and wings tucked away, yet
to unfurl and carry him to the other side
of the Atlantic and back, their love a flash,
an impression, half an image
on a frame of film, waiting to be developed.

—Heather Fee

12. Hold the sea fan inside the frame and mark the placement of the basswood stand. Use a craft knife and the small drill bit to remove at least ⅛" (3 mm) from this square. Glue the fan into place with the Gorilla Glue and let it dry completely.

13. Glue the frame to the base with the Gorilla Glue and weigh it down.

14. Tie the seashells to the sea fan through the top of the interlock snap swivel.

15. Cut small pieces of balsa wood and paint them white. Miter the corners and trim the basswood where it enters the frame. (The balsa wood is easily cut with a craft knife.)

16. Use tacky glue to adhere the balsa and decorative shells.

Finding Inspiration

Throughout this book I've talked about inspiration found through color, surface, found objects, information, and more. This project was inspired by a friendship, combining my treelike find with this friend's family history and her beautiful poetry.

Chapter Five
INSPIRATIONAL TREES: A Gallery of Solutions

Anita Byers, page 98

Janice Lowry, page 101

Each of us faces a challenge when creating a piece of art, and working on a family tree is no different. Whether the challenge is what format we should employ or what medium we should use, the final outcome is based on the answers we choose. On the following pages are beautiful, whimsical, heartfelt, and striking answers to some of these questions. Each artist shown in this gallery was asked to create a family tree of her own design. As artists, they were encouraged to think "outside" the box, to stretch the bounds of expectations. What follows are the surprising and exciting results of this challenge.

The works include photographs, such as in **Anita Byers** heart-wrenching story told through house-shaped pages (page 98) or **Allison Strine's** cheerful house of family photographs (page 106). Some of the works include names only, such as **Barbara Close's** boldly painted tree (page 99) and Lesley Riley's nest-filled tree of more than seventy-five names (page 105). Some hang, such as **Jenna**

Catherine Moore, page 104

Allison Strine, page 106

Beegle's tribute to the women in her family (page 96). Some rest, such as **Michelle Bodensteiner's** thought-provoking three-dimensional tree (page 97). Some even move, such as **Lisa Engelbrecht's** wildly imaginative family mobile (page 100). The artists represented in this chapter specialize in various disciplines, including art journals, paper art, collage, mixed media, photography, and calligraphy. This wide range of expertise, mixed with a passion for creating, offers many different viewpoints and vantages to ponder and explore.

Contemplate how you too might stretch your vision of a family tree, using these unique pieces as an inspirational springboard. Spend time with each project and find something that could be used in your own tree, perhaps a color, a format, or a theme. Take these examples and mold them into your very own creation—your own vision of family.

Jenna Beegle
PAPER ARTIST, DESIGNER

Like great-grandmother, like daughter—or so it seems, looking in to the eyes of four generations of women. Soft colors, smooth ribbon, and textural photographs of birds and nests all work together in Jenna's solution for honoring her more feminine past.

Michelle Bodensteiner
Paper Artist

Michelle's thought-provoking art doll is her solution to tracing her roots. Small photographs glisten on falling leaves under the safe watch of the mother tree and her bluebird. Embellished with crystal leaves and embroidered trim, this lovely doll is firmly grounded to her roots.

Anita Byers
Paper Artist

Anita's creative solutions to telling the story of her father left for dead in a farmhouse at six months old after his mother was killed was an emotional journey. The story of his adoption by family members and the rest of the family tree are told beautifully through old photographs and a house-shaped journal.

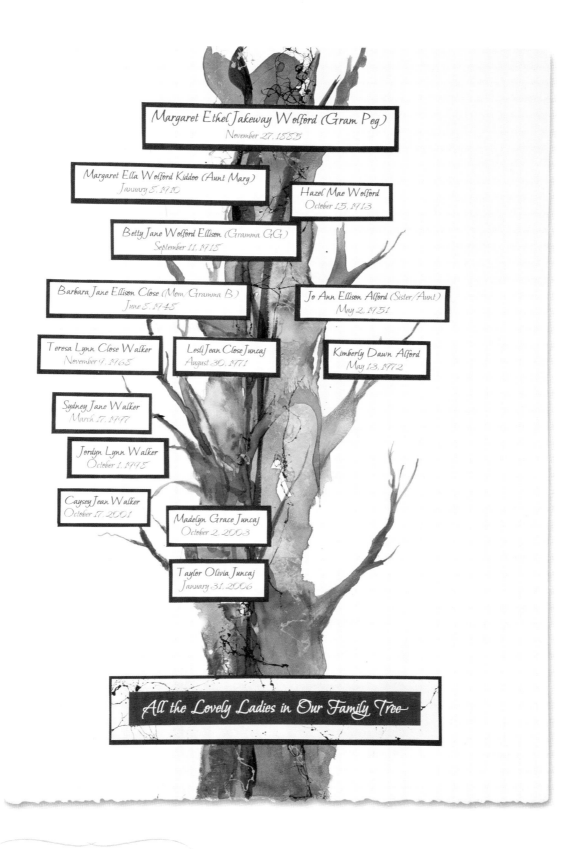

Margaret Ethel Jakeway Wolford (Gram Peg)
November 27, 1885

Margaret Ella Wolford Kiddoo (Aunt Marg)
January 5, 1910

Hazel Mae Wolford
October 15, 1913

Betty Jane Wolford Ellison (Gramma GG)
September 11, 1915

Barbara Jane Ellison Close (Mom/Gramma B.)
June 5, 1948

Jo Ann Ellison Alford (Sister/Aunt)
May 2, 1951

Teresa Lynn Close Walker
November 9, 1965

Lesli Jean Close Juncaj
August 30, 1971

Kimberly Dawn Alford
May 13, 1972

Sydney Jane Walker
March 17, 1997

Jordyn Lynn Walker
October 1, 1998

Caysey Jean Walker
October 17, 2001

Madelyn Grace Juncaj
October 2, 2003

Taylor Olivia Juncaj
January 31, 2006

All the Lovely Ladies in Our Family Tree

Barbara Close
CALLIGRAPHER,
GRAPHIC DESIGNER,
MIXED-MEDIA ARTIST

One of Barbara's signatures is a bold and creative use of color. Here the color serves as her solution for the structure of her family tree. Gouache and pastels pour out across the page, creating a striking balance of words and imagery.

Lisa Engelbrecht
CALLIGRAPHER, MIXED-MEDIA ARTIST

The subtle movement of this mobile enhances Lisa's solution for adding relatives to her family tree. A loose style of hand lettering, sewing, and mixed-media collage shows a heightened sense of fragility and winsomeness.

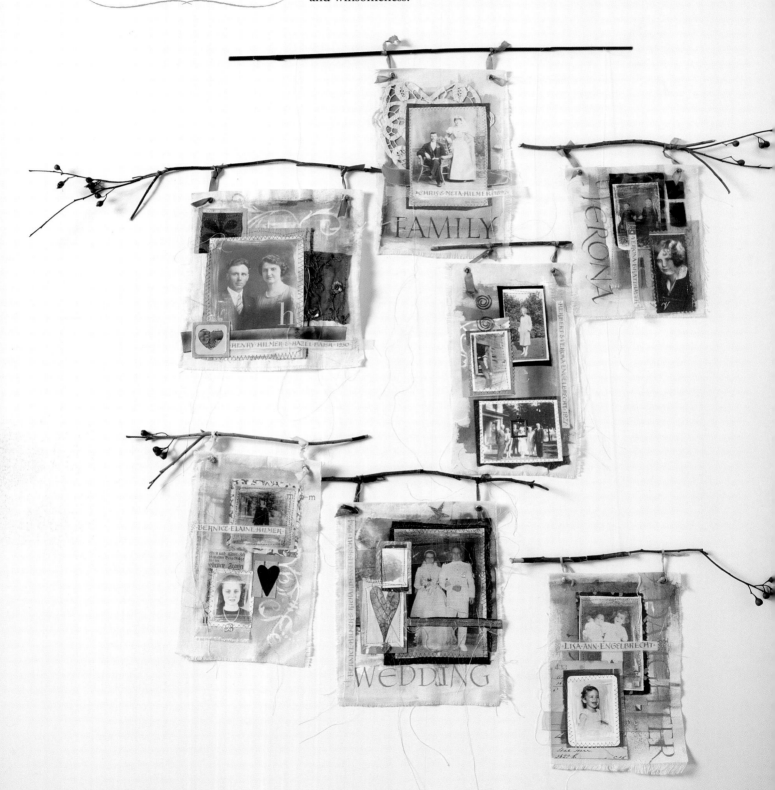

Janice Lowry
ARTIST

A bold approach to a family tree, Janice's piece is reminiscent of cultural reliquaries. Icons, photographs, and found objects are combined to create this family tree and still honor her artistic style.

Stephanie McAtee
PAPER ARTIST, DESIGNER

Stephanie's solution to thinking "outside the box" was to think "inside the compact." An old watch and vintage pearls decorate the outside of this très chic antique compact while the inside is filled with swirling watch parts and family names of four generations of her family.

Karen Michel
MIXED-MEDIA
AND BOOK ARTIST

Focusing on one family member, Karen speaks volumes about where this lovely little boy comes from. With an ancestral background from Germany, Ireland, Haiti, Norway, France, Iroquois, and England and a halo of golden threads, little Nico's story is well told.

Catherine Moore
CONCEPTUAL ARTIST,
DESIGNER

Catherine uses layers of paper, paint, and frames to tell the story of her family. She stays true to her passions by using natural imagery, including trees, birds, and eggs.

Lesley Riley
QUILTER,
MIXED-MEDIA ARTIST

Lesley's solution to creating a large family tree was to take a whimsical approach, using Lutradur for a tree, old fishing net yarn for a nest, and wooden eggs. The eggs have just a slight tint to them, differentiating the boys from the girls, and great-grandchildren grace the piece in the form of beautiful birds.

Allison Strine
MIXED-MEDIA AND
COLLAGE ARTIST

Allison found the solution to creating her family tree in a wooden house and meaningful iconography. She uses small photographs soldered into hanging charms to represent the family members in a joyous and enveloping way.

Lynn Whipple
MIXED-MEDIA ARTIST,
COLLAGE ARTIST,
PHOTOGRAPHER

Lynn's moving piece of family tree art goes deeper than the names and dates of a family and considers where we come from. Small photos hang from string, visually connecting the tree and echoing the statement, "We are all branches on the tree of humanity."

Chapter Six

A Beginner's Guide to Researching

by Tana Pedersen Lord

How much do you know about your parents? Probably quite a bit. But what about your grandparents and your grandparents' parents? Most of us have a strong desire to learn more about the people who came before us—where they were born, who they married, where they lived—and each one of these details gives us a better understanding of what their lives were really like. With a basic knowledge of family history and the right tools, you can be well on your way to discovering more about your family than you thought possible.

Let's Get Started

You may not realize it, but the best place to start your family history is with yourself. Grab a pen and paper, or open a document on the computer and record all the significant events in your life including birth date and place, information about marriage and children, your education, and more. Now it's time to move on to your parents. Record the same types of information for your mother and father. You probably won't know the exact dates for everything. That's not a problem. Include as much information as you know; you can fill in the blanks later. Keep moving backward in time and make a note of any information

Family History

Home Sources

- Announcements for births, weddings, and deaths
- Bibles
- Books with inscriptions
- Certificates
- Church records
- Journals and diaries
- Employment and pension documents
- Estate papers, probate records, and wills
- Family heirlooms such as jewelry and furniture
- Family histories
- Funeral cards
- Insurance and loan papers
- Land records and deeds
- Letters and postcards
- Medical records
- Memoirs
- Military awards, medals, uniforms, and war memorabilia
- Newspaper clippings
- Oral histories
- Passports, visas, and immigration papers
- Photograph albums
- School papers, diplomas, report cards, and yearbooks
- Scrapbooks
- Tax records

you know about your grandparents and even great-grandparents.

Locate Your Home Sources

The next step in learning more about your family is to hunt for "home sources." A home source can be anything from the family bible to the quilt that was sewed by your great-grandmother. Each of these items gives you insight into the personalities of your family members, but they also often contain family facts that you may have never known. A letter from your grandparents may include the names of aunts and uncles and distant cousins; pictures in your mother's photo album may have important dates written on the back. If you don't find any of these items in your home, don't get discouraged. Contact other family members and let them know you're interested in learning more about the family—they just may have the family heirloom you're looking for.

Interview Family Members

Your relatives can be a great resource when it comes to learning more about your family, especially older family members. You can conduct interviews on the phone, in person, or through mail, whatever you're most comfortable with. In addition to finding out important facts and dates, remember to let the individual share the family stories and legends that have been passed on through the generations; these are what truly makes your family unique. Make sure you keep a written record of everything that you learn; you may have to retrace your steps later or you may forget where you learned specific pieces of information.

Set Goals

It's easy to get excited about learning *everything* you can about *every* member of your family tree. However, you will experience less frustration and have a more satisfying experience if you focus your search. Now that you've learned quite a bit about your family, you can use this information and decide what you really want to find out. You might want to set a few long term goals (such as discovering where your great-grandfather was born in France or uncovering the date when your grandfather emigrated from Mexico) and some short term goals (such as finding your father's World War II draft card or your mother's birth certificate). Set a goal now and avoid aggravation later on!

Organize Information

Every time you learn something new about your ancestors, you'll want to record your discoveries. This becomes even more important as you work back in time learning more and more. You can record your information using pen and paper and traditional forms or you can utilize one of many computer software programs made specifically for genealogists.

Charts and Forms

The two basic tools of family historians are the pedigree chart (sometimes called an ancestral chart) and the family group sheet. A pedigree chart shows an individual's direct ancestors:

Types of Records

Think records only exist for births, marriages, and deaths? Check out the variety of records you might encounter:

- *Alumni lists*
- *Biographies*
- *Burial records*
- *Cemetery records*
- *Census schedules*
- *Court depositions and affidavits*
- *Emigration/immigration records*
- *Hospital documentation*
- *Land claims*
- *Military service records*
- *Newspapers*
- *Obituaries*
- *Parish records*
- *Passenger lists*
- *Personal histories*
- *Phone directories*
- *Published family histories*
- *Tombstone transcriptions*
- *Voter registrations*
- *Wills*

parents, grandparents, great-grandparents, and so on. With a quick glance you can see the dates and locations of births, marriages, and deaths for one family line. And, as the name suggests, family group sheets include information about a family group—parents and their children. You'll want to create a family group sheet for each couple in your tree. Free family history charts and forms can be downloaded from various websites. You can find free pedigree charts, census extraction forms, research calendars, and more at Ancestry.com (www.ancestry.com/charts/ancchart.aspx) and FamilyTreeMagazine.com.

Software

Many people prefer to store their family history information on the computer—you don't have to record information in multiple locations, you can print out customized charts, it's easy to share your finds with friends and family, and much more. Some of the most popular software programs are *Family Tree Maker* (FTM), *Personal Ancestral File*

(PAF), *RootsMagic*, and *The Master Genealogist*. Most of these programs have similar features and functionality and all will export your files to GEDCOM format (a universal format that can be opened by any genealogy program). If you don't already have a favorite program, determine how you'll be using the software and choose the product that works best for you.

Make Connections

Before you begin looking for records, you might want to determine if someone has already started working on your family tree. You can save yourself months and perhaps years of work; you might also find a distant relative or connect with someone with whom you can collaborate and share your research.

Message Boards

Message boards are basically electronic bulletin boards. You can post research questions, search for facts about your family, or just learn more about genealogy in general. With more than 20,000 boards on every topic from adoptions to surnames to shipwrecks, RootsWeb.com is a resource that you'll want to take advantage of. And best of all, the message boards are free. You may find a board dedicated to your particular surname or the county where your grandparents lived, or you just may meet people who are willing to share tips that will help you in your pursuit.

Online Family Trees

Another great option to find out whether anyone has been working on your family tree is to look for online family trees. For years, family historians and people just like you have been posting their trees online. You may stumble upon a family tree that matches yours and gain generations of relatives in one search. Some online tree collections are on websites that require subscriptions, such as OneGreatFamily.com and Ancestry.com, while others are free like FamilySearch.org and RootsWeb.com.

A word of warning: not all family trees are equal. An online tree is only as accurate as the person who created the tree. Make sure you evaluate each piece of information and look for sources to back it up before you accept that the material is factual. Remember, these trees are a great resource and start to your research, not necessarily the end product.

Find Your Family in Records

Finally, you're ready to start exploring the world of records—the documents that trace the important events in your ancestors' lives. Records that are considered useful for family history are found in many different places: local, state, and national archives; libraries; cemeteries; churches; and courthouses. Just a few years ago, the only way to access these records was to journey to the old family hometown and hope that the county courthouse would be open *and* have the records you need. Or, you could visit the local library and spend hours examining rolls of film at a microfilm reader. Today, it is much easier to find those all important records.

Online Searches

In recent years, the Internet has become the most important and powerful tool you can use to do your family history. Many records are right at your fingertips and accessible from the comfort of your own home. A variety of records are available online—everything from census records to local phone books. Some websites even have the actual images of the original records; not only does this help you review the information yourself, they're a great way to share your discoveries with other family members. Two of the biggest genealogy websites are Ancestry.com, a subscription site that has millions of records and databases that include billions of names, and Family Search.org, the website of the Family History Library in Salt Lake City, Utah.

Because each website categorizes and indexes (assigns keywords that help identify specific records) their records differently, you'll want to familiarize yourself with each site's search form—make sure you look for search tips, too. Don't worry if you can't find all the records you're looking for in one site, using several different websites may give you the information you're seeking.

On the Road

While the Internet is great tool, some of your ancestors' records will not be found online. You may have to travel to the locations where your family members used to live and search for records in local courthouses, libraries, and archives. Before you make a special trip, determine what days and hours the location will be open, search any available online indexes to find out whether they have the records you're interested in, and make a list of records you plan to find.

Another option is to "send away" for the records. Many records have been microfilmed by genealogical societies, libraries, and other organizations and can be ordered through interlibrary-loan—contact your local library to see if they participate in this kind of lending program. Also, some archives are willing to locate the records you're looking for and mail you a physical copy of the record, usually for a fee. Look for county and state government websites to find information on how to acquire records through the mail.

What Records Should You Start With?

One of the most readily available records online—and perhaps the record that contains the greatest amount of useful and fascinating information is the United States Federal Census. A census is the official count of the population. In the United States, a national census is conducted every ten years. Census records include these types of information: age, sex, race, marital status, literacy, birthplace, and parents' birthplaces; immigration and naturalization dates; military service; occupations and schooling; and much more. There is almost no better way to catch a glimpse of the lives of your ancestors.

The 1930 is the most recent census to be released and is the best place to start your search. Most of us know people who were alive in 1930, whether it's parents, grandparents, or neighbors. If your family was living in the United States in 1930, it's likely that you'll locate at least one family member in these records. The clues you'll find in the 1930 census records can lead you to military records, immigration records and passenger lists, and birth and marriage records.

Good Luck!

With the information and tools explained in this chapter, and an interest in learning more about your family, you will soon be on your way to creating a family tree that you can share with others and treasure for years to come.

Tana Pedersen Lord has been writing and editing in the technology industry for more than ten years and in the field of genealogy for two years. She is the author of The Official Guide to Family Tree Maker *(MyFamily.com, 2006). In the past she has written articles for* Genealogical Computing *and she is currently a contributing editor to* Ancestry Magazine.

Suggested Reading

Calligraphy Books

Want to improve your lettering, or at least take a stab at copying some beautiful letters for a project? These books will get you started.

Calligraphy Alphabets Made Easy
Margaret Shepherd

The Art & Craft of Hand Lettering
Techniques, Projects, Inspiration
Annie Cicale

The Calligrapher's Bible
100 Complete Alphabets and How to Draw Them
David Harris

Genealogy Books and Magazines

Need more information on finding your family history? Try these books and periodicals.

Ancestors
A Beginner's Guide to Family History & Genealogy
Jim and Terry Willard with Jane Wilson

Ancestry Magazine
1-800-ANCESTRY

Family Chronicle Magazine
www.familychronicle.com

Family Tree Magazine
www.familytreemagazine.com

Family Trees
A Manual for Their Design, Layout, & Display
Marie Lynskey

Finding Your Roots
How to Trace Your Ancestors at Home and Abroad
Jeane Eddy Westin

Genealogy for the First Time
Research Your Family History
Laura Best

My Family Tree Workbook
Genealogy for Beginners
Rosemary A. Chorzempa

Organizing Your Family History Search
Efficient and Effective Ways to Gather and Protect Your Genealogical Research
Sharon DeBartolo Carmack

The Genealogy Handbook
The Complete Guide to Tracing Your Family Tree
Ellen Galford

Useful Websites

www.ancestry.com
www.cyndislist.com
www.familychronicle.com
www.familyhistory.com
www.familysearch.org
www.familytreemagazine.com
www.genealogy.com
www.lcweb.loc.gov
www.rootsweb.com
www.usgenweb.com
www.vitalrec.com

TEMPLATES AND CLIP ART

A Layered Family Tree, page 34

Family Group Sheet

Husband _____

Occupation _____

Born (Date/Place) _____

Married (Date/Place) _____

Died (Date/Place) _____

Father _____

Mother _____

Other Wives _____

Wife _____

Occupation _____

Born (Date/Place) _____

Married (Date/Place) _____

Died (Date/Place) _____

Father _____

Mother _____

Other Husbands _____

Children

Sex	Name	Born (Date/Place)	Married (Date/Place)	Died (Date/Place)

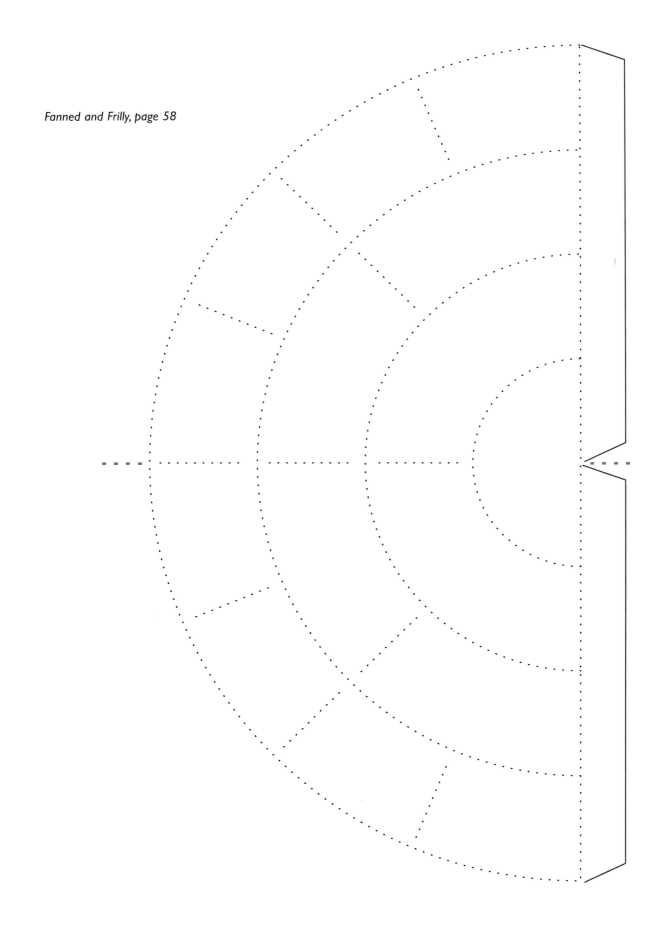

Fanned and Frilly, page 58

NAME

☐ MATERNAL
☐ PATERNAL

NICKNAME

DATE AND PLACE OF BIRTH

SPOUSE AND DATE OF MARRIAGE

DATE OF PASSING

OBSERVATIONS

ARBRE GÉNÉALOGIQUE

Nome de famille : ....

Anniversaire de marriage ....

localisation ....

....

Hiding Jacob's Ladder, page 66

N O P Q R S

shel'drake (shĕl'drāk'), n. [shield + drake.] a Any duck of one of the Old World genera *Tadorna* and *Casarca*, esp. the common European species (*T. tadorna*), slightly larger than the mallard. Though somewhat resembling the geese, its nearest allies are the tree ducks. It frequents coast regions and nests in burrows. It is chiefly black and white, the head and neck greenish, the lower breast broadly chestnut, and the speculum green. The bill with its frontal knob is red. The ruddy sheldrake (*C. casarca*) of southern Europe, Asia, and northern Africa, is chiefly orange brown with the quills of the wings and tail blackish and the speculum bronzy green. The male in summer has a black collar. It is abundant in India, where it is called *Brahmany duck*. Other species of *Casarca* inhabit South Africa, New Zealand, and Australia. **b** Any merganser; also, locally, any of various other ducks.

Sheldrake (*Tadorna tadorna*).

shelf (shĕlf), n.; pl. SHELVES (shĕlvz). [ME. *shelfe, schelfe*, AS. *scylfe*; akin to G. *schelfe*, Icel. *skjalf*. Cf. SHELVE, v. t.] **1.** A thin, flat, usually long and narrow, piece of any material set horizontally at a distance from the floor, as on a wall, to hold objects of use or ornament; a ledge; a long narrow surface, horizontal or nearly so, above a larger one. **2.** Something resembling a shelf or ledge in form or position; as : **a** A sand bank in a river or the sea, or a rock, or ledge of rocks ; a reef or shoal. *Stow.*
On the secret *shelves* with fury cast. *Dryden.*
b A flat, overhanging layer of rock. **c** *Mining.* A stratum with a shelflike surface; bedrock under alluvial soil. **3.** Pieces of timber running the whole length of a vessel inside the timberheads under the deck beams.

shelf'y (shĕl'fĭ), a. **1.** Abounding in shelves; shelvy : a Full of dangerous shallows. "A *shelfy* coast." *Dryden.* **b** Full of ledges ; of flat projecting layers, of rock. *Obs.*

shell (shĕl), n.; pl. SHELLS or, in sense 6, usually collectively, SHELL. [ME. *shelle, schelle*, AS. *scell, scyll*; akin to D. *schel*, Icel. *skel*, Goth. *skalja* a tile, and S. *shell.* Cf. SCALE of fishes, SHALE, SHELL.] **1.** A hard outside covering, as of a fruit or of an animal. Specif.: **a** The covering, the outside part, of a nut ; as, a hazelnut *shell*. **b** A pod. **c** The hard or tough covering of an egg. **d** A hard rigid covering of an animal, commonly largely calcareous, in other cases chiefly or partly chitinous, horny, or even siliceous. The shell of a mollusk consists of one or more calcareous pieces secreted by a modified portion of the surface of the body called the *mantle*, and in typical cases is large enough to cover the animal, but it may be reduced or rudimentary and buried in the soft tissues. A mollusk's shell is enlarged by the deposition of new material, esp. around the edges, to provide for the animal's growth. The shell of a crustacean is the outer chitinous cuticle, often stiffened with calcareous matter. It is molted at intervals to provide for growth, the soft underlying cuticle hardening into a new shell. In the vertebrates having a shell, it is composed of bony plates often covered with horny epidermal shields. **2.** By extension, a shell-bearing mollusk. **3.** Short for TORTOISE SHELL (which see). **4.** Something resembling, or suggesting, or likened to, a shell in some way, as in shape, position, or fragility. Specif.: **a** any slight hollow structure ; a framework or exterior structure that is frail in construction or that has had its interior removed or destroyed, or that is regarded as not complete or filled in ; as, the *shell* of a house. **b** Outside covering, lit. or fig. ; husk ; as, the *shell* of a ship ; the *shell* of religion. **c** The outer frame or case of a pulley block. **d** A coarse kind of coffin ; also, a thin interior coffin inclosed in a more substantial one. *Knight.* **e** A light racing boat, long and only wide enough to accommodate one oarsman on a seat, the frame of which is covered with very thin wood or with paper. Modern shells have outriggers and are decked over except where the oarsmen sit. **f** *Mech.* A thin hollow cylinder, as the barrel of a cylindrical boiler or the knurled outer piece of a kind of drill chuck. **g** The part in a loom in which the reed is fitted. **5.** The copper face of an electrotype. **6.** *Ordnance.* A hollow projectile for cannon, containing an explosive bursting charge which is ignited by a fuse at some point of its flight, upon impact, or after penetration, the effect being produced by the force of explosion or by the impact of its scattered fragments. Shells are classified according to special design and purpose into ARMOR-PIERCING, BLIND-LOADED, COMMON SHELL, DECK-PIERCING SHELL, and TORPEDO SHELL (see these terms). Cf. SHRAPNEL. **7.** A metal or paper case which holds the charge of powder and shot or bullet used with breech-loading small arms. **8.** Something similar in form or action to an ordnance

shell; specif.: a *Fireworks.* A case or cartridge containing a charge of explosive material, as a garniture, which bursts after having been thrown high into the air. It is often elevated through the agency of a larger firework in which it is contained. **b** *Oil Wells.* A torpedo. **9.** An engraved copper roller used in print works. **10.** In a European sword of the 15th century and later, etc., a guard plate, semicircular or nearly so, and sometimes of openwork, attached to the cross guard on either side ; a coquille. **11.** A concave rough cast-iron tool in which a convex lens is ground to shape. **12.** A gouge bit or shell bit. **13.** A stringed instrument of music, as a lyre, — the first lyre having been made, it is fabled, by using a tortoise shell. **14.** *Mil.* Short for SHELL JACKET. **15.** *pl.* Coins ; money. *Old Slang.* **16.** *pl.* The husks of cacao seeds, a decoction of which is often used as a weak cocoalike beverage. **17.** *pl. Med.* Tinted glasses for protection of the eyes. **18.** At several English public schools, an intermediate form or class between the fourth and fifth ; — said to have originated at Westminster School from this form having been taught in a kind of semicircular apse.

shell, v. t.; SHELLED (shĕld) ; SHELL'ING. **1.** To strip, break off, or remove the shell of ; to take out of the shell, pod, etc. ; as, to *shell* nuts or peas ; to *shell* oysters. **2.** To separate the kernels of (an ear of Indian corn, wheat, oats, etc.) from the cob, ear, or husk. **3.** To cover or incase in a shell, lit. or fig. **4.** To throw shells or bombs at, upon, or into ; to bombard ; as, to *shell* a town or a body of troops. **5.** To cover with shells (a surface, as an oyster bed for the spat to adhere to them, or a piece of ground to fertilize it). to shell out, or, rarely, down, to hand out or over ; to pay over (money). *Slang.*

shell, v. i. **1.** To fall off, as a shell, crust, etc. **2.** To cast the shell, or exterior covering ; to fall out of the pod or husk ; as, nuts *shell* in falling ; to be disengaged from the ear or husk ; as, wheat or rye *shells* in reaping. **3.** To use oyster shells, as for culture or fertilizing. *U.S.* to shell out, to hand out or over something demanded, as money. *Slang.* *T. Hughes.*

shell, a. *Mach.* Of a tool, having a through longitudinal hole to receive a bar which is pushed through it and fastened in position ; as, a *shell* end mill, reamer, etc.

shel-lac' (shĕ-lăk' ; shĕl'ăk'), n. Also **shel-lack'**, **shell'-lac'**. [shell + lac a resinous substance ; cf. D. *schellak*, G. *schellack*.] A purified form of lac largely used in the preparation of varnishes. See 2d LAC, n.

shel-lac', v. t.; SHEL-LACKED' (shĕ-lăkt' ; shĕl'ăkt') ; SHEL-LACK'ING (shĕ-lăk'ĭng). To coat or otherwise treat with shellac.

shell'bark' (shĕl'bärk'), n. The shagbark.

shell bit. A gougelike boring tool used with a brace.

Shel'ley's case (shĕl'ĭz). *Law.* A celebrated case of Lord Coke's time (about 1581) which discussed and enunciated the common-law rule (now called the rule in Shelley's case) the effect of which is that when a person receives (by conveyance an estate of freehold with a limitation, either mediately or immediately, to his heirs in fee or in tail, the grantee takes an estate in fee simple or fee tail respectively, the words "the heirs," or "the heirs of his body," having the effect only of limiting the quantity of the estate conveyed. The rule is part of the common law, but in the United States having been very generally abolished or modified by statute so as to give effect to an express limitation of a remainder to heirs.

shell'fish' (shĕl'fĭsh'), n. [AS. *scylfisc.*] a Any aquatic invertebrate animal having a shell, esp. a mollusk, as an oyster or clam, or a crustacean, as a lobster. **b** A trunkfish.

shell flower. a Any cultivated menthaceous plant of the genus *Moluccella*, esp. *M. lœvis.* **b** The turtlehead. **c** The zinziberaceous plant *Alpinia nutans.*

shell gland. *Zoöl. & Embryol.* a In entomostracans and the young of many other crustaceans, a looped tubular excretory organ ending blindly at one extremity and opening to the exterior on or near the second maxilla. **b** In the embryo of many mollusks, a glandular organ which secretes the embryonic shell. **c** A specialized glandular part of the oviduct of many animals which forms the egg's shell.

shell hooks. *Ordnance.* An implement consisting of two arms, for hoisting or moving heavy projectiles.

shell ice. Ice originally formed on a sheet of water, but no longer resting on it, because the water has been withdrawn.

shell'ing, p. pr. & vb. n. of SHELL. Hence : n. **1.** Removal of a shell or shells. **2.** Bombardment with shells. **3.** Groats ; hulled oats ; — a commercial name. **4.** A disease of the grape, of uncertain origin, causing the immature fruit to drop ; — called also *rattling.*

shell jacket. *Mil.* An undress military jacket, tight-fitting, and short in the back, such as is worn in the British army.

shell'-leaf', n. An ornamental Malayan araliaceous shrub (*Nothopanax cochleatum*), with long-petioled, rounded, concave leaves.

shell'man (shĕl'măn), n. **1** *Nav.* A man stationed at a gun to bring a shell and place it in the gun when loading. **2** A swindler who plays the shell game.

shell'proof' (shĕl'proof'), a. Capable of resisting shells or bombs ; bombproof.

shell pump. A simple form of sand pump or sludger con-

sisting of a hollow cylinder with a ball or clack valve at the bottom, used with a flush of water to remove detritus.

shell'y (shĕl'ĭ), a. **1.** Abounding in, or covered with, shells ; consisting of shells, or of a shell. "The *shelly* shore." *Prior.* "His *shelly* cave." *Shak.* **2.** Of, pertaining to, or of the nature of, a shell ; testaceous, chitinous, siliceous, or the like.

Shel'ta (shĕl'tá), n. [Cf. CELTIC.] A secret jargon of Celtic tinkers, and many other, esp. Irish, vagabonds.

shel'ter (shĕl'tẽr), n. [ME. *sheltron, shiltrom, scheltrome, scheldtrone*, a guard, squadron, AS. *scildtruma* a troop of men with shields ; *scild* shield + *truma* a band of men. See SHIELD, n.] **1.** That which covers or defends from injury, exposure, annoyance, or the like ; a protection or place of protection ; a screen ; a refuge.
Thou (God) hast been a *shelter* for me. *Ps.* lxi. 3.
2. State of being covered and protected ; protection.
And their *shelter* takes their tender bloom. *Young.*
Syn. — Asylum, refuge, retreat, covert, sanctuary, protection, defense, security.

shel'ter (shĕl'tẽr), v. t.; SHEL'TERED (-tẽrd) ; SHEL'TER-ING. **1.** To be a shelter for ; to provide with a shelter ; to cover from injury or annoyance ; to shield ; protect ; harbor.
Those ruins *sheltered* once his sacred head. *Dryden.*
2. To screen or cover from notice ; to disguise.
In vain I strove to check my growing flame.
Or *shelter* passion under friendship's name. *Prior.*
3. To place under shelter or protection ; to take or betake to cover, or to a safe place.
They *sheltered* themselves under a rock. *Abp. Abbot.*
Syn. — SHELTER, SHIELD, SCREEN. *Shelter* and *shield* are often interchangeable ; but SHELTER suggests esp. protection from exposure, SHIELD, from assault ; SCREEN, which is often used with little distinction from *shelter*, frequently implies masking or concealment ; as, to *shelter* from stormy weather, to *shield* from impending danger, to *screen* an accomplice. See DEFEND.

shel'ter, v. i. To take shelter. *Milton.*

shelter deck. *Shipbuilding.* A continuous deck of lighter construction than an awning deck, extending fore and aft on the upper deck.

shelter trench. *Mil.* Any trench hastily constructed to secure shelter from direct fire. — usually first a shallow excavation with the dirt thrown up as a parapet in front, to shelter a man lying down, and deepened as rapidly as possible until it will shelter a man standing, if time permits.

shel'ty, **shel'tie** (shĕl'tĭ), n.; pl. SHELTIES (-tĭz). Lying ; Kneeling ; Standing. [Prob. of Scand. origin, perh. influenced in sense by some other word.] A Shetland pony.

shelve (shĕlv), v. t.; SHELVED (shĕlvd) ; SHELV'ING (shĕl'vĭng). [Prob. fr. *shelf* a ledge, a platform ; perh. influenced in sense by some other word.] To incline ; to be sloping ; as, the bottom *shelves* from the shore.

shelve, v. t. [See SHELF.] **1.** To furnish with shelves ; as, to *shelve* a closet or a library. **2.** To place on a shelf ; hence, to lay on the shelf ; to put aside ; to dismiss from service ; to put off indefinitely ; as, to *shelve* an officer ; to shelve a claim ; to *shelve* a matter in debate.

shelv'ing, p. pr. & vb. n. of SHELVE, v. t. Hence : n. **1.** Act of fitting up shelves. **2.** Act of laying on a shelf, or on the shelf ; putting off or aside ; as, the *shelving* of a claim. **3.** Material for shelves ; shelves, collectively. **4.** A detachable rack or framework of boards attached to a farm wagon or cart to increase its capacity for hay or grain ; — usually in the pl. *Chiefly Scot. & Dial. Eng.*

shelv'ing, p. pr. & vb. n. of SHELVE, v. i. Hence : a. A sloping or shelvy place. *Rare.*

shelv'y (shĕl'vĭ), a. Sloping ; shelving.

She-ma' (shĕ-mä'), n. [From the first word of the selection, in Heb. *shĕma'* hear.] A selection of short passages from the Pentateuch (*Deut.* vi. 4-9, xi. 13-21 ; *Num.* xv. 37-41) recited, together with certain benedictions, as a creed or statement of the Jewish faith.

She-mo'neh Es'reh (shĕ-mō'nĕ ĕs'rĕ), n. [Heb. *shĕmoneh 'esreh*, lit., eighteen.] *Jewish Religion.* The collection of 19, orig. 18, benedictions, from which are taken those recited together with the Shema at the daily services and at the additional service on Sabbaths and holy days. The first three and the last three are used at all services, while the middle group varies on Sabbaths, new moons, and holy days from the formula prescribed for week days. The collection as the prayer par excellence is called the *Tefillah* (prayer), and each benediction is called among the Sephardic Jews an *awidah* (i. e., benediction recited standing).

shend (shĕnd), v. t.; SHENT (shĕnt) ; SHEND'ING. [AS. *scendan* to disgrace, bring to shame, from *scand, sceond*, disgrace, dishonor, shame ; akin to G. *schande*, Goth. *skanda*, and E. *shame.* See SHAME, n.] *Obs. or Archaic.* **1.** To blame, reproach, or revile ; to punish, degrade, disgrace, or put to shame or confusion, as by defeat or superiority ; to confound.
The famous name of knighthood foully *shend.* *Spenser.* *R. Browning.*
2. To injure, mar, spoil, or harm ; to ruin ; to destroy. **3.** To protect ; to defend.

shend, v. i. *Obs.* **1.** To be or become injured, spoiled, ruined, or destroyed. **2.** To defend ; to answer in defense. *Destruction of Troy.*

N
O
P
Q
R
S

shield fern. The buckler fern.

shield'-shaped' (shēld'shäpt'), a. Having the shape of a shield; specif., Bot., peltate.

shield'tail, n. Zoöl. Any small burrowing snake of the family Uropeltidae, having a large acute on the tail.

shift (shĭft), v. t., shift'ed; shift'ing. [ME. shiften, schiften, to divide, change, remove, AS. sciftan to divide; akin to LG. & D. schiften to divide, distinguish, part, Icel. skipta to divide, part, shift, change, Dan. skifte, Sw. skifta, and prob. to Icel. skifa to cut into slices, as n., a slice, and to E. shive, shiver, n., shiver, n.] **1** To divide; distribute; apportion; assign; arrange. Obs. or Dial. Eng. **2.** To change the place or position of; to move or remove, as from one place or person to another; to transfer; to turn; as, to shift a burden; to shift the blame.

> Carrying the oar loose, [they] shift it hither and thither at pleasure.   Raleigh

3. To put off; to get rid of; avoid; evade. Obs. Spenser. **4.** To exchange for or replace by another or others of the same kind or class; to change; as, to shift the clothes; to shift the scenes or scene. **5.** To change the clothing of; — used reflexively. Obs.

> Not to have patience to shift me.   Shak.

6. To change in form, character, etc.; to alter. — **to shift off.** a To delay; to defer; to put off. **b** To put away; to lay aside; to get rid of. — **to s. the helm,** Naut., to put the tiller from starboard to port or vice versa, usually from hard over one way to hard over the other.

shift, v. i. **1.** To make division or apportionment; to distribute; to dispose; to order. Obs. Cursor Mundi. **2.** To deal; to act; to do. Obs. Caxton. **3.** To make a change or changes; to change position, place, form, character, clothing, etc.; to move; veer; to substitute one thing for another; as, the cargo shifted.

> Into the lean and slippered pantaloon.   Shak.
> Here the Baillie shifted and fidgeted about in his seat. Scott.

4. To resort to or use expedients; to provide, look out, or do, for one's self; to contrive; to manage; to manage to live or get along; as, to shift for one's self. **5.** To practice indirect or evasive methods. **6.** Music. To make a shift. See SHIFT, n., 3.

Syn. — See CHANGE.

to shift for one's self, to provide or care for one's self.

shift (shĭft), n. [See SHIFT, v. t.] **1.** Act of shifting. Specif.: **a** A putting one thing in place of another, or changing the place of a thing; change; alteration; substitution.

> My going ... was not merely for shift of air. Sir R. Wotton.

b A turning from one thing to another; a turn; hence, an expedient or scheme tried in difficulty; often, an expedient that is petty, mean, underhand, or the like; a trick; a dodge; a fraud. "Reduced to pitiable shifts." Macaulay.

> I 'll find a thousand shifts to get away.   Shak.

2. Something changed or used in alternation; esp.: **a** A change of clothes. **b** A woman's chemise. **c** A shirt. Dial. **3.** Music. A change of the position of the hand on the finger board, in playing the violin or a similar instrument. The first position of the hand is close to the nut, so that the first finger produces the tone next above that of the open string; at half shift, or second position, the hand is so moved that the first finger falls in the original place of the second; at whole shift, or third position, the first finger covers the original place of the third; and at double shift, or fourth position, it covers that of the little finger. **4.** Mining. A dislocation of a vein or seam; a fault. **5.** The change of one set of workmen for another; hence, a spell, or turn, of work; also, a set of workmen who work in turn with others; as, a night shift. **6.** In building, shipbuilding, etc., disposition of work overlapped so as to break joint.

Syn. — See EXPEDIENT.

shift of crops, change or rotation of crops.

shift'er (shĭft'ẽr), n. One that shifts; specif.: **a** One that changes the place or position of something; as, a scene shifter. **b** One given to resorting to shifts or expedients, esp. those of a petty or crafty nature; a cheat.

> 'T was such a shifter that, if truth were known,
> Death was half glad when he had got him home. Milton.

c Naut. An assistant to the ship's cook in washing, steeping, and shifting the salt provisions. Rare. **d** Mach. Any of various devices for shifting something; as: (1) A belt shifter. (2) Knitting Mach. A wire for changing a loop from one needle to another, as in narrowing, etc.

shift'ing, p. pr. & vb. n. of SHIFT. Hence: n. Philol. Lautverschiebung;— **shift'ing-ly,** adv.

shifting accent or **stress,** Phon., variable word accent, or stress, due to unsettled or varying usage, to the position of the word with reference to other words, or to the exigencies of verse. Thus, Eng. farm'yard'; Amer. farm'yard'; an out'side' passenger, the passenger out'side', etc. See Guide to Pron., § 57. — **s. backstays,** Naut., temporary stays to be let go when the vessel tacks or jibes.— **s. center** or **centre.** = METACENTER. — **s. stress.** See SHIFTING ACCENT. — **s.** or **secondary, use,** Law, a use which takes effect in derogation of some other estate and is expressly limited by the deed or may be created on a certain contingency by a per-

shield'drake' (shēl'drāk'). Var. of SHELDRAKE. Scot.
shield'er, n. One who shields.
shield'less, a. See -LESS.
shield'less-ly, adv. — shield'less-ness, n.
shiel'drake (shēl'drāk'). Var. of SHELDRAKE. Scot. [hut.]
shiel'ing. Var. of SHEALING.
shieps. + SHEEP. [SHY.]
shi'er (shī'ẽr), a., compar. of shy. shi'er (shī'ẽr), n. Also shy'er. A horse given to shying.
shiere. + SHIRE.
shies (shīz), n., pl. of SHY.
shi'est, a., superl. of shy.
shift'a-ble, a. See -ABLE.
shift'ful, a. Full of resource. Obs. [SHIFTY.]
shift'i-ly (shĭft'ĭ-lĭ), adv. of SHIFTY.
shift'i-ness, n. See -NESS.
shiga-ga'ion (shĭ'ga-gī'on). See SHIGGAION of the Heb. shig-gā'ion (shĭg-gā'yon). Var. of SHIGGAION. [Heb.]
shih. + SHEE.

Golden Shiner (Abramis chrysoleucus)

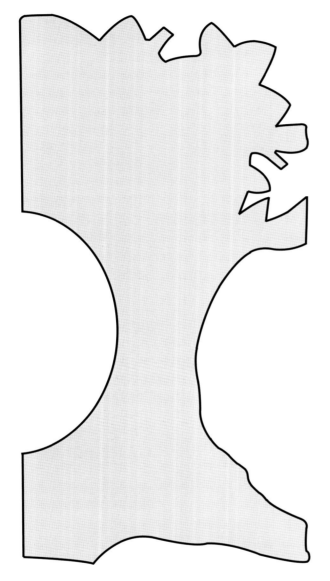

Tree template

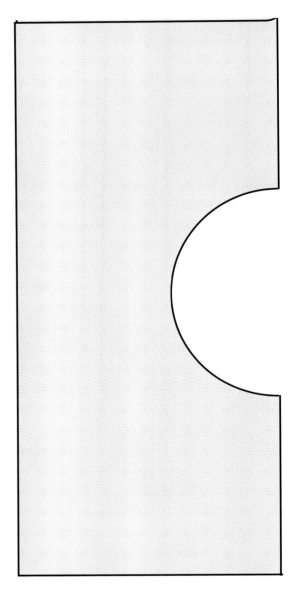

Window template

RESOURCES

Most of the tools and supplies used in this book can be found at your local paper, art, or craft supply store as well as hardware and home improvement stores. See the list below for some of these well-known chains. For those products that I especially like to use or that I know may be hard to locate, I've listed some resources below.

Acrylic Glazes, Mediums, Fluid Acrylics, Molding Pastes, Gessoes, and Grounds
I really enjoy using Golden brand supplies for my work because I can trust the quality and can easily combine products together. They are also well known for their customer support.

Golden
www.goldenpaints.com

Black Writing Marker
I love to use my Pigma Micron pens in all sizes. I use the very tiny 005 all the way up to the 08.

Sakura
www.gellyroll.com

Blending Marker and Wintergreen Oil
Both used for toner-based image transfers, the blending markers can be found at art supply stores and the oil at health food stores.

Chartpak
www.chartpak.com

Aura Cacia
www.auracacia.com

Comb Painting Tool
This tool is made by a number of manufacturers. The one used in this book was made by Plaid and is called a Multi-Purpose Comb.

Plaid
www.plaidonline.com

Curly Willow Branches
These can be found at florists and also import stores.

Pier One
www.pier1.com

Disc Binding Punch
The binding system used in this book is Rollabind.

Rollabind
www.rollabind.com

Eyelet Setting Tools
I like to use the Home Pro tool by American Tag because the eyelets look finished on both sides. You can also use it to punch holes in sturdier papers and boards.

American Tag
www.americantag.net

Inks
Ranger makes a great array of dye-based inks including their Distress Inks. Tsukineko's StazOn ink pads come in many colors, both opaque and nonopaque, and are fast drying and suitable for stamping on glass, metal, plastic, and more.

Ranger
www.rangerink.com

Tsukineko
www.tsukineko.com

Inkjet Printable Fabric
A number of paper companies make printable fabric. I like the selection available from The Vintage Workshop.

The Vintage Workshop
www.thevintageworkshop.com

Metal Trellis Form
These trellises or topiary forms can be found at home improvement centers in the garden department. For a larger variety of forms try Bloomingdoor.

Bloomingdoor
www.bloomingdoor.com

Optometrist Lenses
These lenses can be found in many paper art stores and at antique and flea markets.

The Shoppe at Somerset
www.stampington.com

Paper and Millinery Flowers
These can be found at many different antique shows and specialty paper stores. Most of the flowers used in this book came from Paper Source.

Paper Source
www.paper-source.com

Sea Fan
The sea fan used in this project was found at a nautical-themed booth at the Brimfield Fair (see Antique Shows and Markets, page 131). You can order one online as well at Naples Sea Shell Company.

Naples Sea Shell Company
www.naplesseashellcompany.com

STORES

It just may be impossible to list all the fabulous local stores with art, paper, and craft supplies in one book, but I'll get you started with some of my favorites in the U.S.

Arizona—Gilbert
Ink It! Inc.
Located in the historic district of downtown Gilbert, Ink it! is an uncommon store that celebrates it uniqueness in classes, products, and atmosphere. They are used to catering to the mixed-media artist too. As the exclusive onsite store for Art Unraveled, they know their stuff.
225 N. Gilbert Road
Gilbert, AZ 85234
480.632.6801
www.inkitinc.com

California—Santa Ana
The ARTbar
This eclectic shop is located in the Santa Ana Artists Village and is known as the hands-on mixed-media studio where everyone is an artist.
209 N. Broadway
Santa Ana Artists Village, CA 92701
714.558.2445
www.theartbar.net

California—Lake Elsinore
A Little Bizaar
If you can judge a store by its workshops, then A Little Bizaar is a superstar. They offer a "unique selection of cool, funky, unusual, fantastic, and wondrous items."
31712 Casino Drive #5B
Lake Elsinore, CA 92530
951.471.0882
www.alittlebizaar.net

California—Los Angeles
Sweetpeas and Snapshots
This unique store is a true destination spot. It's *the* place to have a bridal or baby shower, birthday, or tea party if you love paper and all the accoutrements like I do.
11726 W. Pico Boulevard
Los Angeles, CA 90064
310.479.2444
www.sweetpeasandsnapshots.com

Colorado—Boulder
Two Hands Paperie
Location, location, location, Two Hands is adjacent to the Pearl Street pedestrian mall in Boulder. This store is a treasure trove of paper-related products and is great place to shop at for items you didn't even know you needed.
803 Pearl Street
Boulder, CO 80302
303.444.0124
www.twohandspaperie.com

Maryland—Savage
The Queen's Ink
Fabulous supplies and wonderful guest instructors—Queen's Ink has got it going on!
Savage Mill Box 2048
8600 Foundry Street
Savage, MD 20763
301.497.9449
www.queensink.com

Massachusetts—Boston
Rugg Road Paper Co.
Located on a charming street in good old Boston, Rugg Road is a great stop to pick up paper and other unique items.
105 Charles Street
Boston, MA 02114
617.742.0002

Massachusetts—Great Barrington
Off the Beaded Path
This charming store is like hitting two birds with one stone. Off the Beaded Path is a hip store with an eclectic selection of beads and jewelry-making supplies and embellishments of all kinds. A great work-
shop space and a sister/owner dynamic duo make this a great place to shop. Did I mention the disco ball and the secret play-room for the kiddos? You may go in for the embellishments but you'll go back for the vintage bracelets, and the beads, and the paper, and the … .
67 State Road Unit 1B
Great Barrington, MA 01230
413.528.6111

Massachusetts—Somerville
Spark Craft Studios
A new concept in retail store and work-shop space, they offer wine nights on Fridays and tea on Sundays. Paper craft, beading, knitting, and crochet are all among the topics they serve.
50 Grove Street
Davis Square
Somerville, MA 02144
617.718.9132
www.sparkcrafts.com

Massachusetts—Topsfield
Absolutely Everything
This is a paper arts store with the latest merchandise and special classes in book arts and collage techniques featuring artists from around the country.
30 Main Street
Topsfield, MA 01983
978.887.6397
www.absolutelyeverything.com

Michigan—Ann Arbor
Hollander's
Hollander's specializes in decorative papers, bookbinding supplies, and work-shops. Their list of workshops will impress anyone, and with more than 1,200 papers in stock to choose from you'll be hard-pressed to leave without buying some-thing magnificent. If you make the trek to Hollanders, make time for a delicious lunch at Zingerman's Deli at 422 Detroit Street and then take a walk around the

beautiful University of Michigan campus.
410 N. Fourth Avenue
Ann Arbor, MI 48104
734.741.7531
www.hollanders.com

Michigan—Royal Oak
The Stamping Grounds
A tiny store located in the trendy town
of Royal Oak is filled to the brim with
stamps, tools, supplies, and embellishments. It never fails—I never leave without a handful of must-haves.
228 W. Fourth Street
Royal Oak, MI 48067
248.543.2190
www.stampinggrounds.com

Missouri—St. Louis
Red Lead Paperworks
Red Lead is another gem of a store with
no shortage of papers and embellishments. I just love a store that inspires me
while I shop.
10041 Manchester Road
St. Louis, MO 63122
314.822.8288
www.redleadstl.com

North Carolina—Apex
Artists' Oasis
"Quench your creative thirst" is their
motto and by golly you can do just that
in this store, both literally and figura-
tively. (They have a tea room where you
can sit and browse reference books!) Is it
fair to say that I give a paper store more
credit when they carry some of my
favorite supplies such as Golden paints?
1000 N. Salem Street
Apex, NC 27502
919.367.9933
www.artistsoasis.com

Antique Shows and Markets

I am a sucker for farmers markets and
antique fairs (and really great yard sales).
Because there was no fruit or vegetable
injured in the making of this book, I'll
skip over the list of my favorite farmers
markets and touch on a few outstanding
antique and yard sales.

Brimfield Antique and Collectible Fair
This is by far my favorite place in the
country to make a yearly pilgrimage.
Actually, I can trek there three times a
year now that I live back in
Massachusetts. They have a show every
May, July, and September. Check their
website for this year's dates.
www.brimfieldshow.com

Warrensburg Garage Sale
Touted as the world's largest garage sale,
this is the place to come and find anything! Antiques, hard-to-find items, old
toys, new toys, hats, hardware, vintage
clothing, handmade crafts, dollar items
are all listed as items you might find at
this yearly (late September) garage sale,
flea market, craft fair, food fest, and bargain hunter's dream in upstate New York.
www.warrensburggaragesale.com

The World's Longest Yard Sale (aka
the 127 Sale)
This sale is so large it's been on HGTV
and the *Tonight Show* and featured in
*Southern Living, Country Living, USA
Today*, and *Newsweek*. It takes place
every year during the beginning of
August and runs 450 miles from
Gadsden, Alabama, to Covington,
Kentucky.
www.127Sale.com

Chain Stores

When you can't find what you need at
your local store you can almost always
count on finding it at one of the bigger
chain stores. Below are some of those to
look for in your area or online.

Australia
Eckersley's Arts, Crafts and Imagination
www.eckersleys.com.au

Canada
Michael's
www.michaels.com

United Kingdom
HobbyCraft
www.hobbycraft.co.uk

United States
A.C. Moore
www.acmoore.com

Dick Blick
www.dickblick.com

Hobby Lobby
www.hobbylobby.com

Michael's
www.michaels.com

Paper Source
www.paper-source.com

About the Contributing Artists

Jenna Beegle

Jenna Beegle used to spend her time creating with needle and thread before discovering the joys of paper crafting. Starting with scrapbooking, her paper crafting career has been more varied and interesting than she could have expected. Jenna works for Anna Griffin, Inc., creating lovely things, in addition to teaching stamping, scrapbooking, and altered techniques, and more recently knitting. Jenna's work has been seen in *Memory Makers, Legacy, Somerset Studio,* and *Paper Crafts* magazines.

Michelle Bodensteiner

Michelle Bodensteiner is a freelance paper artisan from Loveland, Colorado. Her love of paper and art came from early childhood but took focus in 1999 when she was introduced to rubber stamping. She has since been published in national rubber stamp magazines, has taught stamp art classes in her locale, was a participating artist for a book art exhibit at the Loveland Museum Gallery, and is currently doing design work and art for B Line Designs in Mustang, Oklahoma. She lives with her husband, Chris, her high-school sweetheart and companion of forty years.

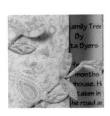

Anita Byers

As a child Anita Byers remembers designing clothing and purses and learning to craft from her grandmother. After a lifetime of dabbling in a number of art forms, she finally found her niche—collage—at The ARTbar in Santa Ana, California, and now dares to collage anything that exists.

Barbara Close

Barbara Close is a freelance calligrapher, graphic designer, and instructor. She teaches calligraphy and mixed-media workshops and classes across the country. She is a

member of the Society for Calligraphy, Southern California, and currently is serving as past president and public relations chair.

Her work can be seen in Glen Epstein's calendars, the Artful Letter Calligrapher's Engagement Calendars and SfC's Artful Book of Days Calendar. She has exhibited her work in several juried shows and has designed several greeting cards for Marcel Schurman Company. She has designed the logo for *Somerset Studio* magazine, where her work is often featured, and is their lettering consultant.
barbicl@aol.com
www.bcdezigns.com

Lisa Engelbrecht

Lisa Engelbrecht combines letters, collage, stitchery, and fabric together in a fearless way. A traditionally trained letterer, professional calligrapher, instructor, and a freelance artist for American Greetings, Lisa pushes the boundaries of lettering arts.

She was named successor to her mentor Marsha Brady at the Cerritos College Calligraphy Program where she implemented a certificate in calligraphy. She has been on the faculty of seven International Lettering Conferences.

Lisa teaches at numerous conferences and her work is featured in *Artist's Journals and Sketchbooks* (Quarry Books) and *Beyond Paper Dolls* (Stampington & Company), both by Lynne Perrella, and *Quilted Memories* (Sterling/Chapelle) by Lesley Riley. She is a frequent contributor to *Somerset Studio* and her work has been featured on the covers of *Legacy* and *Quilting Arts* magazines.
lengelbrecht@earthlink.net
www.lisaengelbrecht.com

Heather Fee

Heather Fee has a master of fine arts in poetry from Naropa University in Boulder, Colorado. She likes to write on the border between poetry and fiction and live on the border between cultures. Originally from the Chicago area, she teaches English as a second language and creative writing in Barcelona, Spain.

Janice Lowry

Janice Lowry was born in Phoenix, Arizona, where her art influences were roadside shrines and a mixture of Mexican, cowboy, and religious art. She attended Art Center College of Design in Pasadena, California, receiving her bachelor of fine arts and master of fine arts degrees. She creates every day in her studio in Santa Ana, California.
www.janicelowry.com

Stephanie McAtee

Stephanie McAtee lives in Kansas City, Missouri, and has always had a passion for journaling and photography. She enjoys using dimensional and interactive elements in her art. She hopes to draw people into her work to embrace the whole piece—and get it. Her hope is that one day her boys, Bobby and Ethan, will look at her work and know what she was thinking and feeling and understand the depth that she put into her art. The boys are her subjects that she's "crazy in love with."

Karen Michel

Karen Michel has studied at the School of Visual Arts in New York City and at the Institute of American Indian Arts in Santa Fe, New Mexico. She is a professional artist, painter, book artist, and teacher, and is founder of Creative Art Space for Kids, a nonprofit organization on Long Island, New York. She travels and teaches workshops across the country, and has been widely published in books and art and craft magazines. She lives in Island Park, New York.

Catherine Moore

Catherine Moore is a conceptual artist, designer of Character Constructions rubber stamps, and an art instructor based in Peachtree City, Georgia, who is best

known for her metaphors on family and nature. Birds, eggs, feathers, and nests are the foundation of her visual language.
www.characterconstructions.com

Lesley Riley

Best known for her Fragment series of small fabric collages, Lesley Riley is also an internationally known teacher, quilter, and mixed-media artist with a passion for color and the written word. Her art takes the form of art quilts, fabric books, dolls, and more. Her art and articles have appeared in numerous publications and juried shows. She is the arts editor of *Cloth Paper Scissors* and author of two books, *Quilted Memories* (Sterling/Chapelle) and *Fabric Memory Books* (Lark/Chapelle), which takes bookmaking in new directions.
www.lalasland.com

Allison Strine

By day, Allison Strine is a happy mixed-media/collage artist whose exuberant creations have won awards and appeared in national arts magazines. At night she's a not-very-good cook, a wife to a left-brained husband, and a tucker-inner of two joyful children.
allisonstrine@mac.com

Lynn Whipple

Lynn Whipple is a Florida native and mixed-media artist who shares her life with her artist husband, John, and their two cats. For sixteen years they each have had work spaces at McRae Art Studios, a warehouse with twenty-five other artists. Lynn draws, paints, photographs, collages, sews, dips things in wax, writes, and uses found objects in assemblage. She has always been fascinated by history, old books, lost letters, worn fabrics, family photographs, wooden boxes, and odd pieces of memorabilia.
www.whippleart.com

About the Author

Jenn Mason is a fine artist, author, teacher, designer, and consultant who loves getting her hands dirty. Happier peeling dried gel medium off her fingers than getting a manicure, Jenn splits her time between creative pleasures and creatively raising her two daughters with her husband. She enjoys traveling across the country and abroad through her writing and classes. Jenn also spends her time designing products and consulting to companies within the paper arts industry. When the girls are in school and there are no deadlines looming you can find her blissfully painting in her Brookline, Massachusetts, studio.

You can reach Jenn through her website www.jennmason.com

Other Books by Jenn Mason

Pockets, Pullouts, and Hiding Places
Interactive Elements for Altered Books, Memory Art, and Collage

Paper Art Workshop
Handmade Gifts
Stylish Ideas for Journals, Stationery, and More

Paper Art Workshop
Celebrating Baby
Personalized Projects for Moms, Memories, and Gear

ACKNOWLEDGMENTS

And, because my mum always told me to remember my pleases and thank yous …

I could not have created this book without the help of many family genealogists, especially Dad, Aunt Edna, Aunt Moldy, Aunt Dorothy, and Missy. Thanks for passing the torch and sharing the stories.

Thank you to all of the art contributors for your brilliant additions to this book. And thank you Heather for your moving poetry. I'm so glad fate has a sense of humor and brought you back into my life on the outside of a petting zoo.

Thanks again to Matt, who once again suffered through lame dinners, a messy house, and a shortage of clean underwear. I can't believe you keep letting me write these books!

To my little girls who are just learning to read:

Thank you, Becky and Abby.
I am sorry it took so long.
Let's go to the park now!

To everyone who feigned even the slightest interest in the book as I excitedly expounded on its virtues and my daily triumphs—thanks for listening.

Thank you Mary Ann, Rochelle, and Winnie for the chance to work on this book—I enjoyed EVERY minute! And kudos to Dawn for making it look so good and Tana for her genealogical expertise.

Lastly, to Jen, Kirsten, Vicky, Heather, Deb, Amy, Jennifer, Linda, Barb, and Martha, the women who inspire me no matter where I live.